THE DIRECTOR'S CIRCLE BOOK FOR 2004

The Johns Hopkins University Press gratefully
acknowledges members of the 2004 Director's Circle
for supporting the publication of works such as
The Artisan of Ipswich.

Alfred and Muriel Berkeley · John J. Boland
Alberta Gamble · Jack Goellner and Barbara Lamb
Charles and Elizabeth Hughes · Peter Onuf
Douglas R. Price · Anders Richter · David Ryer
R. Champlin and Debbie Sheridan
Robert L. Warren and Family

The Artisan
of Ipswich

Craftsmanship and Community
in Colonial New England

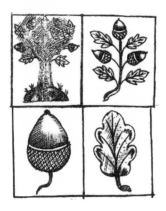

Robert Tarule

The Johns Hopkins University Press

Baltimore and London

© 2004 The Johns Hopkins University Press
All rights reserved. Published 2004
Printed in the United States of America on acid-free paper

2 4 6 8 9 7 5 3 1

The Johns Hopkins University Press
2715 North Charles Street
Baltimore, Maryland 21218-4363
www.press.jhu.edu

Library of Congress Cataloging-in-Publication Data
Tarule, Robert.
The artisan of Ipswich : craftsmanship and community in colonial
New England / Robert Tarule.
p.   cm.
Includes bibliographical references and index.
ISBN 0-8018-7869-1 (acid-free paper)
1. Handicraft—Massachusetts—Ipswich—History—17th century.
2. Artisans—Massachusetts—Ipswich—History—17th century.
3. Artisans—Massachusetts—Ipswich—Biography.   4. Joinery—
Massachusetts—Ipswich—History—17th century.   5. Workmanship—
Massachusetts—Ipswich—History—17th century.   6. Ipswich
(Mass.)—Biography.   7. Ipswich (Mass.)—History—17th century.
8. Ipswich (Mass.)—Social conditions—17th century.
9. New England—History—Colonial period, ca. 1600–1775.   I. Title.
TT25.I67T37 2004
745.4'0974'09032—dc22
2003023184

A catalog record for this book is available from the British Library.

Contents

Preface

Things I Should Have Learned as a Boy

Fresh from graduate school, where I had spent six years studying medieval comparative literature and left A.B.D., I took a teaching job at a small college in Vermont. My wife and I were fortunate to buy an early-nineteenth-century hill farm: a circa 1840 farmhouse, three barns, a large shed, and 100 acres of land, 75 of which were woodlot. Many of the old families were letting go of their property in those days, and we could afford the farm on our modest teachers' salaries. Our nearest neighbors, a few hundred yards away, were an elderly brother and sister—Walter and Lizzie—two of more than a dozen siblings, ranging in age from fifty-five to seventy-five. They had all been born and reared in what was then only a cellar hole in an overgrown clearing about half a mile behind our property.

Walter Potter had worked the woods all his life. He had felled and skidded; he still got his firewood from his own rough land with his twenty-year-old horse. We slowly became neighborly. He had information; I had a young back. I also had an accessible woodlot, an old Ford tractor, and a two-wheeled cart that held a quarter of a cord. I offered to let Walter cut his firewood in our woods with me. His knowledge was my pay. So we spent many hours together in the woods. He would watch me fell a tree and would follow it with his eye as it hung up on a neighboring one, still attached to its stump. Then he would help me safely get it down. By the time it was on the ground, I would know what I had done wrong. He had not told me; he would just let me ask the right question.

In my early thirties I was taken by an urge to build my own house with my own hands. Of course it had to be a timber frame building—I was, after all, a scholar of the past, even though I knew no one who had done such a thing. I was confident I would figure it out; it would be a tangible result of all the research skills I had developed during too many years of higher education. One day in the woods I felled a large and nearly perfect white pine tree. It fell right where it should have, and I began to remove the limbs. Partway up the trunk a small gray birch about 3–4 inches thick lay bent in an arc, pinned by the pine. Too quickly I cut through the birch, and I could see the severed end of the small tree, its elastic energy released, coming straight at my head. Instinctively I put my left hand up, even though it still held the saw. Then I was sitting down, the still-running saw having grazed my left knee. Inside the cut I could see the top of the femur and kneecap. I was working with another fellow in the woods that day, and he drove me out on the tractor and got me to the ER, where they patched my knee with twenty stitches. I had been lucky and only lost skin. When I went back to the woods to retrieve my chainsaw, I saw that the top of the gas tank had been staved in. The little birch tree had hit the saw (better that than my head) and driven it into my knee.

I described the accident to Walter. Of course I knew why it had happened. The small birch was under tension, and I, in too much of a hurry, was not standing to the side. Walter told me about a fellow he had known, or heard about, who felled a small white ash tree about 8 inches thick. Ash is well known for sometimes splitting up the trunk as it falls. The fellow knew this and had his horse about twenty feet behind the tree. The ash split and speared his horse through the stomach. A few weeks later I showed Walter the scar on my left knee. He examined it and then rolled up his left pant leg: he had an identical scar, the same length, in the same place.

Walter is long dead now, but I realized that I learned more from him than from any adult before. I had gone to the best eastern schools, secondary, college, and graduate. I had read widely and was conversant in a good handful of dead languages. But somehow school, all twenty years of it, had not been about life. Walter, as accomplished and wise in his world as any of my academic teachers were in theirs, showed me useful things—how to milk a cow, raise calves and beef, slaughter, and butcher; how to make a fence; how to make hay; how to be a neighbor. But more important, Walter showed me how to work.

The small college fell into financial difficulties about a decade after I began to teach there, and I was laid off. By then I realized that my future lay in some sort of combination of history and hands-on. I was fortunate to get a position at Plimoth Plantation, the living museum of the *Mayflower* passengers, as curator of Mechanick Arts, responsible for the wooden aspects of the replica Pilgrim village. I did research, made things myself, and trained others. After a few weeks at the job I realized that the material world of the Pilgrims—the tools, materials, and techniques—was what the English call postmedieval and that there I was, ten years out of graduate school for the study of medieval literature, figuring out some of the lost secrets of the seventeenth-century woodworker. True, the social world of the Pilgrims was early modern, but how they lived and worked was not far removed from the social world of their medieval ancestors.

Eventually I decided that I needed to complete my doctorate, so I enrolled in the Union Institute, where I was permitted to do something as a historian no conventional program would have allowed: to make, as the centerpiece of the dissertation, a piece of furniture and to let the process of making drive the research. The project was a combination of all I had learned in school about making sense of the written text with all I had learned in the woods with Walter about the intelligence of physical work. Out of that work came this book.

I owe thanks to many people. At some point while I was curator at Plimoth Plantation, my manual skills finally caught up with my academic skills, and I figured out how to transfer what I had learned at the academy about methods of scholarship and proof to the world of common wooden objects. I had been riving oak and cedar fencing and clapboards for about a year at the Plantation when Robert Trent walked me through the seventeenth-century furniture collection at the Museum of Fine Arts, Boston, and showed me curious signs of shrinkage in some of the wooden pieces. To him I owe my first insight (and many more) that the seventeenth century joiner worked in green wood. How to replicate the techniques began to become clear in my mind's eye. I am indebted to my woodworking colleagues at Plimoth Plantation—Joel Pontz, John Sullivan, Charles Cann, and Ted Curtin (who later became my furniture making partner)—for the benefit of their company. We were all more or less infected with the fever of the chase and we all knew that many eyes were better than two. Like many others,

I owe a special thanks to Abbott Lowell Cummings, who trusted me to raise a replica of the 1636 Dedham, Massachusetts, Fairbanks House on Boston Common as part of the city's 350th anniversary in 1980 and to raise it again two years later for the "New England Begins" exhibit at the MFA, Boston. A decade later, he agreed to be on my doctoral committee. Thanks also to Robert St. George, my other committee member, who shared with me his research on Thomas Dennis to get me going. I've many thanks for my friends in the timber framing community: Ken Rower and Ed Levin, who made the Fairbanks Project work, and to Preston Washburn and Michael Burrey at Plimoth Plantation. Also at Plimoth Plantation, Marie Pelletier in graphics, blacksmith Mark Atchison, and Peter Follansbee, a fellow joiner, helped me see in many different ways. I thank my acquaintances in England, furniture specialists Victor Chinnery and Peter Russell and botanist/historian Oliver Rackham, to whom I owe a special debt. Particular thanks to our English friends and hosts, Jack and Brenda Lewis of Somerset. My thanks go to the owners of the furniture, both the private individuals and the museums and their patient curators, who all gave me easy access to their Dennis pieces for study. In particular I need to thank James Kyprianos, at the time resident caretaker of the Ipswich Historical Society's Whipple House, for his generosity in giving me frequent access to their Dennis chest and in sharing everything he knew about Ipswich. And thanks also to Winterthur Museum for the study grant in residence they awarded me in 1990, during which time I organized my research on Dennis. I must thank John Demos for bringing my dissertation to the attention of Robert J. Brugger at the Johns Hopkins University Press; and to Bob I offer special thanks for his tact and patience in helping me turn something unwieldy into this book. Rex Bradeen helped me with the artwork for the book. To family—Shara, Guy, and Lincoln—goes thanks for forbearance during the times that the book came first. And to Jill, my wife, who bore the greatest inconvenience, this book is dedicated.

A Note to the Reader: English currency in the seventeenth century was made up of pounds, shillings, and pence (£, S, and p). Twelve pence made a shilling, and 20 shillings made a pound. It is very difficult to come up with accurate equivalencies to modern money, but the standard day's wages for an artisan during this time, 3 shillings, provides a rough touchstone.

If we assume that a skilled worker today makes $25 per hour, or $200 per day, then the cost in Ipswich of a two-wheeled cart, about 3 pounds, drawn either by a horse, about 5 pounds, or a team of two oxen, about 12 pounds, means that the light-duty horse cart cost $10,500 in today's money, and the heavy-duty ox cart cost about $20,000—not too far from what a light-duty automobile and a pickup truck cost now.

The language in the quotations from the *Ipswich Town Records* contains the original spelling and punctuation, although symbols representing words have been expanded. The language in other quoted material follows the system of the modern author or editor.

In the seventeenth century the new year did not begin until March 25. I have placed dates between January 1 and March 24 in the previous year to conform with modern practice.

The engravings at the beginning of each chapter are from Randall Holmes's *Academy of Armoury,* a late-seventeenth-century English work illustrating the various things that might be found in a coat of arms.

All photographs of the Ipswich Historical Society's chest are by Ted Curtin, as is the photograph on page 45.

The Artisan of Ipswich

Introduction

I F   F U R N I T U R E   C O U L D   T A L K , what might it tell? What would be at the heart of its story? The chest shown on the following pages is a kind of furniture called joinery, and the artisan who made it more than three hundred years ago had apprenticed in the trade. Joinery, the common method of making furniture in England in the sixteenth and seventeenth centuries, came to the New World with the English settlers in the seventeenth century, when an English-born joiner made this piece of furniture in New England.

The chest is in the standard pose, the one you will usually find in a home or a museum gallery or in books on furniture. The first thing you see is the carving. A design covers the whole front, the public face. The joiner's great skill as a carver lay in the panels, the three wide pieces that make up the front of the chest. He knew just where to put the ruler and the compass to begin to divide the space. He had a great number of inherited, traditional shapes that he could arrange and rearrange in many ways while keeping the design immediately recognizable to his customers, most local and many of them neighbors. His carving shows great technical skill and a solid mastery of his tools. He was at once the composer and the musician. Not only did he design and execute the carving, but he made the chest as well.

Now look at the back, the side toward the wall that nobody ever

THE FRONT OF THE CHEST

The chest is typical of the work of the joiner: many smallish pieces of wood are fixed together to make the frame, and panels of thin wood fill the spaces. This chest front is made up of two stiles, two horizontal rails, two muntins running between the rails, and three panels filling the spaces. Eight pinned mortise and tenon joints hold the pieces together. The front is covered with an elaborate carving that catches the eye.

THE REAR OF THE CHEST

The front of the chest was the public face—the rear was not meant to be seen, and here the joiner often used pieces of wood not good enough to be seen on a visible face. The left-hand muntin has a large knot on one edge, the panels are beveled quickly, the right end of the top rail is narrower than the left, and the surface is bare wood, free of paint, oil, or wax.

examines. The back is made like the front. There are two legs (properly called stiles), two long horizontal rails, and two short vertical muntins, which connect the rails and separate the three panels. The skill of the carver is obvious on the front, the public face. Here on the plain, unseen back the craft of the joiner shows clearly, from the trees he chose to fell to how he split, worked, and finished the green oak. The "secret" that lay at the core of his trade was the draw-bored mortise and tenon joint, an ancient development of wide adaptability.

Every place where two pieces of wood come together on the frame there is a mortise and tenon joint. Wooden pins hold each joint tightly together, just as pins pull the massive pieces of a timber-framed barn together. One can see where the joiner's plane tore the grain of the wood and the layout lines he scratched to locate the mortises. But there is more to see back here. There is the forest. Part of the joiner's craft included splitting a log to get these pieces, such that the tree's yearly growth rings lie square to the surface. You can read the tree's life like a book: each ring is a year. And you can see a muntin with a big knot where a branch once grew; the joiner could not use it on the front, so he put it back there, against the wall, where no one would care. He wasted little.

When you look the chest all over, you see equally the hand of the artisan and the hand of nature: by dint of tradition, experience, and skill, the joiner formed the oak of nature into an object of human utility. Nature shows on the back, where the revelations of the grain tell much about the land. The carving on the front is an act of craft over nature: the carving obliterates the wood, rendering it but a surface. Further, the new chest sported bright vermillion and black paint on the background of the carving, making the wood look even less like wood.

In America, the heyday of joined furniture was the seventeenth century. Since relatively little joined furniture was made in the sparsely populated New World, however, Americans now are unfamiliar with its appearance. To the present-day English, joined furniture is a common sight. When the craft of joinery came to New England, it was already an ancient technique, its roots going back several millennia to the Iron Age, when artisans finally had sharp, durable tools and began to explore fully the ways in which wood could be used. New World joiners, who themselves split their timber from a log, were practicing the simplest of timber conversion

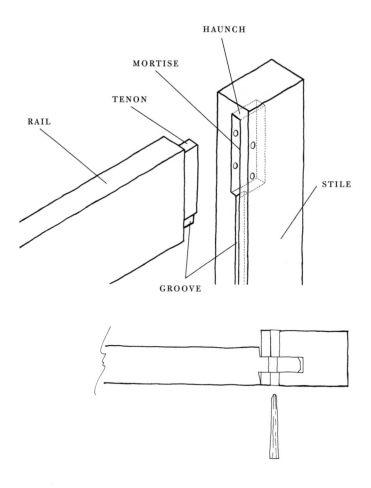

HAUNCH

MORTISE

TENON

RAIL

STILE

GROOVE

THE MORTISE AND TENON JOINT AND THE DRAW BORE

Top, An exploded view reveals how the top of the mortise is set a short distance below the top of the stile. The haunch allows the mortise to keep its structural integrity. The grooves in the stile and on the underside of the rail receive the panel. *Bottom,* A section through a pin, showing how the draw bore works. The pin, in attempting to line up the backs of the offset holes, forces the tenon tightly against the stile. A pin removed from a draw-bored joint retains the bend it took on as it did its work. The effect is entirely mechanical; glue was never used.

technologies. Saws able to slice logs end to end into boards and planks did not appear until the Roman Empire; and sawmills, which used water power to move the hand sawyer's saw up and down, not until the Middle Ages. Like many early technologies, joinery as practiced in the New World was labor-intensive, while the raw materials were relatively inexpensive. Throughout New England, joiners used local wood, mostly oak, to make furniture that was, for the most part, used locally.

Furniture historians have mainly been interested in the visual appearance of a piece of furniture—form, decoration, and finish—and have concentrated their investigations on the point of view of the client who purchased the furniture new. Such investigations have led to a thorough knowledge of the sequence of furniture styles and to the interiors in which the furniture lived. But there are other things to find in furniture. This joined chest, because of the direct processing of local materials and the highly visible craft of the joiner, can illuminate the local landscape, the community in which it was made, and the artisan who made it in his shop.

Chapter One

Ipswich

THE CHEST ILLUSTRATED in the introduction was made toward the end of the seventeenth century in the Massachusetts Bay Colony town of Ipswich, a long day's sail north of Boston. (It is now an hour's drive.) Captain John Smith, who sailed the New England coast in 1614 and published a report of his trip in 1616, provides the first European description of Ipswich, which he called by its Indian name, Angoam (present-day Agawam). The future Ipswich "might content a right curious [careful] judgment; . . . Heere are many rising hills, and on their tops and descents many corne fields, and delightful groues. On the East, is an Ile of two or three leagues in length; the one half, plaine marish grasse fit for pasture, with many faire high groues of mulberrie trees and gardens; and there is also Okes, Pines and other woods to make this place an excellent habitation, beeing a good and safe harbor."[1]

Smith's report of New England might be the first in print, but European fishermen had known of the abundant cod on the Grand Banks off New England for centuries—word of mouth spreads quickly and widely among seagoing men. By the sixteenth century French, Spanish, Portuguese,

Basque, and English fishermen regularly came in summer to catch that fish. The fishermen made temporary camps along the shore from Maine to Massachusetts, where they preserved the fish by drying them on wooden platforms. At the end of the summer, their dried cod salted and packed in oak barrels, they returned to their home countries. In the early 1600s several attempts at permanent settlement failed. Not until the two hundred *Mayflower* passengers disembarked at Plymouth, Massachusetts, on Christmas Day 1620 did a permanent English settlement take hold in New England. No new English settlements were attempted in the New World for about a decade, until, finally, the "great migration": between 1629 and 1643 roughly twenty thousand English—men, women, and children—mostly middle-class yeomen, frustrated by difficult economic conditions at home, made the arduous passage across the North Atlantic.

The *Mayflower* passengers, after difficulties organizing financial backing and finding ships, did not sail until the middle of the summer, late in the year for a westward Atlantic passage. Headed for Virginia, the *Mayflower* first sailed west to Massachusetts, making landfall on the tip of Cape Cod. But the captain, probably wisely, feared the late fall storms and treacherous waters known to lie south of Cape Cod, and he refused to sail south. Plymouth, with its small but secure harbor, sufficed to protect the ship until spring. Some aboard the *Mayflower* had wanted to go on to Ipswich, which the captain had visited previously, but winter was closing in. Half of the passengers, with no shelter and little food, died that first winter.

The immigrants of the great migration, however, a decade after Plymouth, were well organized and well financed. When the English settled a new site, they sailed from England in the early spring and had enough time to plant a food crop and build simple shelter before winter. Often the first English to arrive in a New England town were from the same part of England; recruitment and organization tended to be regional. But, perhaps more significant, England had several different systems of farming. In the New World it was important to agree quickly on how to proceed, and farmers from different systems found it hard to work together.

The two chief systems were the enclosed field and the open field. In an enclosed-field system, each farmer owned his own lands; his house was either on the farmland or in a small hamlet. Enclosed fields tended to be small, and hedges, impenetrable to cattle, separated adjacent fields. An enclosed-field farmer acted as an individual. Enclosed farming predominated in East Anglia, and farmers there practiced two distinct forms of agriculture: the raising of sheep and production of wool on the one hand and, on the other, the raising of crops for the London market, easily accessible by water. An East Anglian farmer was used to making farming decisions based on market demands and decided for himself whether a field was pasture, hay, or tillage and what and whether to plant or whether to leave a piece fallow.

In an open-field system the main unit was the village, small and densely built. The typical village was surrounded by three large common fields. Each farmer owned a long, narrow strip, each about a day's plowing, in each field. All the farmers met regularly to decide how best to treat each field: was it pasture or hay, crop or fallow? And they all had to agree, since only the perimeter of the open field was secured against cattle, and it would not do for someone to be grazing cows or sheep right next to someone attempting to grow wheat or barley. An open-field farmer acted as a member of a cooperative group.

In 1643 the great migration abruptly ended. Economic conditions had improved in England; opportunities at home seemed better than the uncertain dangers of emigrating. For the rest of the seventeenth century only a handful of new settlers came from England, and the first generation's children and grandchildren accounted for most of the increase in New England's population, from about 25,000 by 1650 to 100,000 by 1700.[2]

Settlement Patterns

Ipswich was not among the first coastal sites settled by the English. The harbor was fairly small, and the last few miles up the Ipswich River were difficult at best. Strong tides, erratic winds, and shifting sandbars made the approach risky for large, oceangoing ships, so the English preferred to establish their first settlements in places where the harbors could accommodate larger ships—Salem in 1629, Boston in 1630. In the early 1630s, the English in Boston, the administrative and economic center of the Massachusetts Bay Colony, feared that the French, who were active in the Canadian New World, might attempt to settle nearby. Agawam, despite its attractions, was still empty. In March 1633, John Winthrop, the Puritan leader of Boston, sent his son, John Jr., there with twelve men to establish a town. The English had long known of the agricultural potential of the place, and fear of a French settlement so near to Boston finally overrode the disadvantages of the safe but small harbor. The first year, the men built shelter, began to farm, and determined the boundaries of the village.

Sailing up the Ipswich River from the open ocean, one came, in about 3 miles, to the harbor, a quarter mile long but only a few hundred feet wide. The village began at the harbor. Here, protected from the open ocean, the town developed a range of sea-based economic activities: wharves, warehouses, shipyards, and saltworks, where seawater was turned into salt, a necessity for the preservation of food. About half a mile upriver from the harbor lay a shallow bay of about 3 acres, at the end of which lay the small Lower Falls. Although not big enough for large ships, the bay was adequate for canoes and small boats. About one quarter mile upstream of the small falls lay a larger set of falls, up to which the Ipswich River was tidal. At this set of falls—known as the Upper Falls—the first grist-mill (for grinding grain into flour) in town was built, and by the end of the seventeenth century both falls supported a number of grist- and fulling mills (for finishing wool cloth) and a sawmill. Between the harbor and the Upper Falls a number of artisans—coopers, blacksmiths, ship carpenters, and tanners, among others—lived and worked. A short distance above the Upper Falls was a natural ford across the river. The town had built a foot-bridge by 1635, but not until the mid-1640s did the town build a bridge able to support cart traffic.

The original town center, where the house lots clustered, was roughly triangular in shape, about a mile on a side. Most of the village lay north-west of the river. One side followed the river from the harbor upstream past the ford, a second ran west from the harbor, under a long, steep hill; the third side returned from the western end to the river above the Upper Falls. In the middle of the triangle, at the top of a low hill surrounded by the majority of the house lots, the town built the meetinghouse, a structure that served as the spiritual, civil, and military center. Agricultural land and woodlots lay immediately beyond the original village bounds, the backyard fences of the last houses. To the south of the town were a number of hills, probably the cleared ones mentioned by Smith. About 4 miles to the south of Ipswich the Chebacco River flowed into the ocean, and here grew a second population center, called Chebacco in the seventeenth century but now known as Essex.

In 1634 the first large group of English settlers arrived at Agawam. The colony had already named the new town Ipswich, after the port city in the east of England from which many of the Boston settlers had sailed. From its founding in 1633, Ipswich distributed its land in a way that was usual practice in the earliest English communities in Massachusetts: a town granted house lots in a central village along with some nearby agricultural land to settlers as they arrived and held the rest of the land, some for grants to future settlers and some for the use of the commoners.

England planned thoroughly for the organizing and settling of its New England colonies in the 1630s. Groups of prominent individuals obtained from the king of England a charter, which gave them rights to settle a particular region. Ipswich fell into a grant for the northern half of present-day Massachusetts; Boston lay at the southern end of the grant. Several grants were combined to form the Massachusetts Bay Colony. In England, the grant holders organized immigration to their New World holdings. But once settled, the New World towns were largely responsible for their own administration. Colony business was handled by the General Court, a legislative and judicial body. The General Court, in turn, elected a governor. Membership in the General Court and the right to vote for members were limited to the freemen, a select group. To be a freeman, one had only to be a member in good standing of the colony's established church. There were no requirements of inheritance, wealth, or landholding.

In the first few years of the Massachusetts Bay Colony all business was handled in Boston, but as the towns developed in the 1630s, the General Court let them handle their affairs. In 1636 the General Court established four regional courts with a jurisdiction between that of the town and that of the colony, and one of these courts met in Ipswich. In 1643 the General Court set the boundaries of the counties, and each county in the colony had its own court, which met quarterly in several towns in the county. In Essex County, courts were held in Salem and Ipswich. These courts handled town matters, leaving the General Court in Boston free to deal only with colony matters.

The settlement of Ipswich followed the typical colony pattern. The

MAP OF IPSWICH AND ENVIRONS

The village harbor was several miles from the ocean; upstream the river was not navigable, and downstream lay much marshland. In the seventeenth century the town of Ipswich included the settlement of Chebacco, which later became a town in its own right. Although it was about 10 miles by water from Chebacco to Ipswich, much wood was brought from the well-wooded Chebacco to the village of Ipswich and to the many artisans who worked there. *Inset,* Ipswich as situated on the coast of Massachusetts Bay Colony.

Atlantic Ocean

PLUM ISLAND

HOG ISLAND

IPSWICH VILLAGE BOUNDS

DENNIS HOUSE

X

WILLIAM FELLOWS FARM

THOMAS DENNIS'S TREES

CHEBACCO (ESSEX)

IPSWICH

SALEM

Atlantic Ocean

BOSTON

10 MILES

WEST MEADOWS

GRAVELLY BROOK

TIMBER HILL

BUSH HILL

IPSWICH RIVER

THICK WOODS

TO HAMILTON

1 MILE

General Court and the governor granted the right to settle to groups of freemen. In Ipswich, freemen elected a group called the Seven Men (by midcentury called the selectmen) and a number of town officials, who together conducted town business. The selectmen, with the approval of the freemen, distributed land to new settlers.

Many New World towns looked much like all open-field and many enclosed-field counterparts in England: the villages, where most people lived, were densely built and surrounded by farmland. In the New World, this familiar arrangement had the added advantage of offering security from a century-long series of conflicts with the Indians. In the first decade of Ipswich's settlement the town granted a number of house lots in the village, most to husbandmen (farmers), artisans, and fishermen, people of only modest wealth. Ipswich also had a number of wealthy and prominent settlers, whose lots were scattered throughout the town. The right of commonage in Ipswich went only with these house lots in the village. The house and lot could be sold, but the right of commonage stayed with the house lot and belonged to the new owner. For most of the century there were about two hundred Ipswich commoners. The commoners met regularly to decide how to use the commons, within broad limits set by the freemen and selectmen.

In Ipswich, the number of commoners was much larger than that of freemen. Freemen were generally, but not always, commoners, but many commoners were not freemen. An Ipswich commoner could vote on the business of the commons but had no voice in town or colony business. By far the greatest number of those who lived in Ipswich were "inhabitants." Neither freemen nor commoners, they had no voice in colony, town, or common-land business. All three groups—freemen, commoners, and inhabitants—paid rates (the seventeenth-century term for taxes) to both colony and town.

Most Ipswich village lots were only a few acres each, and on them the owner built a dwelling house, agricultural buildings, and often a shop, if he was an artisan. Along with the house lots, the town gave small grants of outlying land for planting and for cutting hay. A typical small grant to a husbandman or artisan was about a dozen acres, six of plow land and six of hay land, enough to provide for much of his family's food but not much more. The size of these grants usually reflected the economic standing of the immigrants: the more well off, the larger the grant.

The status of commonage included several rights. An artisan could plant a few acres to crops in the common fields; graze domestic animals in the common pasture; cut hay from the common meadow; and cut trees for fuel, fencing, and building materials and for his trade. Many artisans owned no farmland, just a lot in the village and rights to the resources of the commons. Almost everyone had a cow and maybe a calf, and the more established artisans had a horse for carting. The domestic animals and the agricultural resources of the commons formed a contained system: the animals' manure fertilized the ground that grew crops, whether vegetables on the house lot in the village or field crops—wheat and rye, Indian corn, root crops, cabbage, flax—in the plow land outside the village.

Ipswich also gave a few large parcels of land, often in the hundreds of acres, as an inducement to wealthy and influential individuals to settle in town. Indeed, towns sometimes bid for these prominent immigrants. With these large grants also went the right of commonage, not for the farm itself but for a separate house lot in the village. Through much of the century the town required the large landowners to own a dwelling in the village, in part for safety and in part to be near the meetinghouse and its moral and civil authority.

Responsibilities also went with the right of commonage: the building and maintaining of the fences that kept livestock from the land used as plow land and hay land, and adherence to the town's regulations, which specified how to graze the town's livestock and fell the town's trees. Ipswich artisans, like artisans in other rural towns, farmed much of the summer and worked at their trades in the winter. The busiest farming times of the year were planting, haying, and harvesting; between April and September there might be time for artisan work, but not much.

A New Artisan Comes to Ipswich

Thomas Dennis, the joiner who made the chest illustrated in the introduction, was an Ipswich commoner. An average sort of fellow, he was neither rich nor poor. Born in England in 1638, Dennis immigrated to New England in 1663, at the age of twenty-five. He was a fine artisan, and his carving, many say, was the best done in the seventeenth-century New World. From the carving on the furniture he is known to have made, it is clear that he apprenticed in Devonshire, in southwestern England. Growing up he saw the local style of carving everywhere—on furniture, on the pews in church, on buildings in the town. As a child he unconsciously absorbed the traits of his predecessors, the people who had taught his master's masters. Dennis worked in a local vernacular tradition whose visual grammar he knew fluently. He had a complexity and variety of design— traits his New England–born sons would not have—that could come only from an acquaintance begun in childhood, practiced in adolescence, and used in adulthood. For Dennis, comfortable with his materials, techniques, and design, no two pieces were ever exactly the same.

Dennis's work, like that of all artisans, was public. Houses, barns, mills, vehicles, storage containers, footwear, farming machinery, and furniture were all made locally. Dennis's work had to meet not only the standards of his trade but also the careful eyes of his neighbors, who could drop in on him in his shop. His work had to be strong and neat, and his designs had to please. Dennis never signed his work; no seventeenth-century furniture maker did. Everyone in Ipswich would have recognized his work. In a time before factories, which separated the maker and the process of making from the user, a town's necessary daily goods were made nearby, and neighbors kept everybody honest.

With documents we can read a story, connect the dots of Dennis's life, and create a coherent image. Dennis's furniture, in the same way, can tell a story—how he got his oak, where the trees came from, how he carefully made the piece; indeed, we can see the several thousand years of woodworking experience that provided the craft within which Dennis worked. To see Dennis's furniture, we will have to begin with the trees that yielded the timber that Dennis used, a subject that was common knowledge to his Ipswich peers but is much less visible to us.

Dennis knew wood at a cellular level. He also knew the smallest workings of the town. The other Ipswich artisans understood their material as well as Dennis did his. Dennis and his fellow artisans were bound by the public nature of their lives and work. They were also bound by the trades they practiced and their common bodies of traditional knowledge, passed from one generation to the next by the apprenticeship system.

In New England, as in England, formal apprenticeship began at fourteen, roughly the age of puberty, and lasted until twenty or twenty-one.

An apprentice learned his master's physical habits: how to hold a tool, how to put his body behind it. He also learned mental habits: the sequence of the work, how one visualized the object, consistent measuring and marking. Once learned, these "habits of workmanship" were used by the artisan throughout his working career, not because they were better than anyone else's (they all met the same high standards) but because to work otherwise could have slowed him down. Mental systems, hard-wired into the brain, made the work go more smoothly by relieving the artisan of the need to think, that is, to be aware verbally of his work. He knew where a tool lay on the bench, how to hold it and apply it to the work, what to do with the other hand, what to do next—all this he could do without a thought. But add a different tool, or a new step, and the old patterns could be broken and slowed, which could lead to mistakes.

Besides guiding the apprentice in the "mysteries" of the trade, the master was contractually bound to teach the young man to read, write, and do math (at least enough to keep accounts) and to instruct the youth in Christian virtues. The public school, if a town had one, was mostly for the children of the elite. Artisans were schooled at home, albeit someone else's. By the age of twenty-one, a young man had completed his apprenticeship and become a journeyman, which meant that he could work for another master for wages. An apprentice was not paid but received room, board, and clothing. At the end, the master typically gave him a suit of clothes and a set of tools. A young artisan married only when he had become a journeyman or, if he was a farmer, after he had acquired enough land to farm.

Manual traditions learned through apprenticeship tended to endure (ever try to unlearn a "bad" habit?), and the work of the apprentice looked like the work of the master at the level of the smallest details. Shop traditions in many trades have been identified using this assumption. In seventeenth-century New England, regional traditions were a step beyond a given shop, as the second, third, and fourth generations spread out geographically: different shops in a region were rather like first cousins. But all was not stasis. There was change, but as with language, it occurred slowly from generation to generation.

Some trades, like cooperage and wheelwrighting, probably changed little in their appearance: their first purpose was function. But other trades, like joinery and carpentry, were susceptible to changes in taste, like those Dennis's children would experience toward the end of the seventeenth century and the beginning of the eighteenth. The work of Dennis and his sons might have looked different over time but at the level of the small details was probably similar, so long as the technology remained the same. Dennis was the last generation of furniture makers to work primarily in oak in the New World. To understand the knowledge he brought with him from England, a look at oak in the Old World is required.

Chapter Two

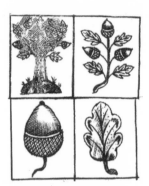

Oak:
The Material of Choice

THOMAS DENNIS brought to Ipswich an ancient understanding of oak, a wood long associated with the workings of civilization in England. Six thousand years ago in the southwest of England, late Stone Age farmers used oak boards split from logs to make walkways through wet areas. They clearly knew many of oak's virtues: that freshly felled it split readily, that it was of immense strength when dry but worked easily when green, that it rotted very slowly, and that it grew to great size. But stone tools, which tended to shatter when struck, were unsuited for any complicated wood-working, and not until the Iron Age—about three thousand years ago—did tools appear in northern Europe that could effectively work wood. The Celts, who came to the British Isles about five hundred years later, were soon making buildings, farm implements, and complex cart wheels from oak. The Romans arrived in the first century B.C., bringing with them a long knowledge of the technical uses of oak, from which they made ships, buildings, barrels, and, in London, wharves. Thomas Dennis could have picked up the tools of the Roman woodworker—saws, planes, chisels, and hole-boring tools—and gone easily to work. In the fifth century A.D., colonizing Anglo-Saxon tribes from the east brought their own northern European oak-using traditions. They built dwellings from oak boards cleft from trees and set vertically. Viking boatbuilders a few centuries later planked their seagoing vessels with oak cleft from trees and set horizontally.

Artisans and farmers used other trees, too, for particular uses. Beech and ash were about as hard as oak but rotted easily if damp; they found use indoors for tools, equipment, and machinery. Sawyers turned elms and many softwoods into boards, some of them very wide, since these trees grew to large size. Hazel of a few inches in diameter was made into all sorts of fencing about the farm. And rot resistant chestnut, introduced to England by the Romans, was the chief wood for fencing where it grew, and in oak-poor parts of England it substituted for oak in timber frames.

But premodern England was unique in northwestern Europe: no large softwoods—no pines, spruces, and firs—grew there. Scots pine was one of the first trees to grow in England after the glacier, but by historical times it grew in useful numbers only in the Scots Highlands and as a timber tree was almost unknown to English woodworkers. As sea level rose, the land bridge connecting France with England became the English Channel before the softwoods now common in Europe spread north, and in England oak became the only choice for many artisans. From the Middle Ages on, England, short on supply, traded for timber woods with the Continent. Much oak came from the Baltic countries to Holland, where the Dutch sawed it on wind-powered sawmills. The best sort—wide, clear, sawn oak suitable for making the sides of a farm wagon—was known in England by the Dutch word *wainscot*, which literally means "wagon side."

Besides oak's wide use as a timber, the bark was valuable for tanning leather. Workers could peel oaks only in the spring, when the sap first ran; the rest of the year the bark sticks tight to the wood. Sometimes the cutters removed the bark all the way to the small branches while a tree was still standing, but generally the branches were debarked after the tree had been felled. Finally, the English valued oak as a fuel. One of the best firewoods, it burned slowly with great heat. All the virtues of oak—for man-ufacture, for fencing, for tanning, and for fuel—meant that all oak trees had a use. It even had value as a food; the annual crop of acorns fattened swine before the customary fall slaughter. Oak was rather like the proverbial use-ful pig: one could use everything but the squeal.

England, in the early seventeenth century, was an old agricultural land-scape. The island was blessed with rich soils and a benign climate. Stone Age farmers lived in England for several thousand years and began to de-velop the landscape the New England settlers knew. Most of the land's features—the woods, forests, and hedges; the pasture, meadow, and plow land; and the roads—had been there since the Middle Ages, and many of them had already existed for a thousand years or more. Almost all the English landscape is the direct result of human activities. But the landscape, once established, in turn defines the scope of human activities. The Domes-day Book of 1086, William the Conqueror's inventory of taxable England, indicates that trees covered only about 15 percent of English land, once almost completely forested. By the Black Death in 1349, the figure was 10 percent, as it was in the seventeenth century. Over the centuries such a small amount of woodland had great implications for the wood-using technologies of England, from building to fuel. Complex legal and social conventions grew up around the use of, and access to, what few resources there were.

Wood and Craft in the Old Country

Medieval artisans knew almost all the ways of growing and harvesting trees that their seventeenth-century counterparts knew. Indeed, some methods of woodland management go back into prehistory. For many centuries prior to the settling of North America, the English managed their woods inten-sively. Well before the close of the Middle Ages, they developed the system of woodland management they retained up until the twentieth century: the coppice with standards. Coppices are small parcels of wood-growing land, generally a few tens of acres; some are often no more than a few acres. The word *coppice* comes from the French verb *couper*, "to cut," a technique that takes advantage of the particular vitality with which many hardwoods regenerate themselves after being felled: a single tree will sprout multiple

COPPICE WITH STANDARDS

This English coppice is maintained in the old way. Every seven years or so the understory is completely cut. Piles of straight rods, one of the most important of the coppice crops, lean against a standard tree of typical form. The oak's short trunk is straight and free of branches, which can grow only above the height of the mature understory, 15–20 feet high. In the foreground are several stools, the multistemmed trunks of the felled understory. A single stool can have upwards of fifty individual sticks. The stools covering the ground are so close together—8–10 feet apart—that a few years after harvest, the coppice floor will be completely shaded by them. Composed from several photographs by the author.

trunks. A standard is a tree left to grow larger and become timber for a building, ship, bridge, or other large structure. The whole coppice but for the standards was felled at once. In historical times the English have cut coppices on a five- to twenty- or twenty-five-year rotation, depending on the species of tree and its uses, and invariably in the winter or early spring. Because of the energy provided by the established root system, a coppice shoot grows much faster than does an individual shoot grown from seed.

The English made an important distinction between timber and wood. Timber was large and the stuff of construction, as in timber-framed buildings, and wood was smaller, from poles to brushwood, as in firewood. A common dividing size was 8 inches in diameter at the stump. Anything over was timber; anything under, wood. The distinction occurs in the medieval Latin records and was significant to the seventeenth-century residents of Ipswich, Massachusetts.

For the English coppice owner the greatest income came from the sprouted wood, called underwood or smallwood, and not from the large timber trees. The English used hazel rods of 1–2 inches in diameter, the result of a five- to seven-year harvesting rotation, for fencing and for building, as well as for some specialized craft activities. An acre of hazel coppice could grow five thousand such small poles. A twenty-year rotation, for trees other than hazel, produced wood of 4–6 inches in diameter. The English used some of these larger poles in construction and around the farm, but much of this wood they burned as fuel. This fuelwood also produced good charcoal, which in some areas was the chief coppice crop. Since the underwood represented the greatest value, the English did not allow the standard or timber trees to grow so closely together that their shade adversely affected the growth of the underwood. Twelve standards per acre was sometimes used as a suitable number, but it varied more or less in practice. Every harvesting of the underwood they might leave a few particularly straight and healthy young trees, called staddles, that would replace the standards over time.

Besides the coppice with underwood and standards, there were several other ways to grow trees, and each method produced its own sort of wood and timber and had its own characteristic landscape. In England, as around the world where the various systems of agriculture developed, the richest lands were used to grow vegetable and grain crops, the next grew hay, the next provided pasture, and the poorest land was left to grow wood. Much of the oldest agricultural land in England, on the light and fertile chalky soil of the south and southeast, was the least wooded. In Kent and Sussex, the presettlement forest—the wildwood—disappeared by Roman times, and numerous, small irregular fields bounded by hedges covered the rolling hills. At some point, probably in Anglo-Saxon times, the inhabitants started to exploit hedges as sources of fuel, fencing, and timber, especially in those areas with few woods. They treated the hedges as though they were coppices and felled a hedge completely at a single cutting. The hedge yielded the same range of products as a coppice, including timber trees. In large parts of England, hedgerow standards provided the local supply of timber for building, and the crowns of trees, which spread even more widely than coppice standards, produced many of the particular, oddly shaped and crooked pieces required for shipbuilding, some of which must possess a right-angle bend.

In addition to trees growing in woods and in hedges, the English used a third, widespread system of growing trees on agricultural land: wood-pasture. In wood-pasture regions, the inhabitants permitted the wide spacing of trees or groups of trees, so that adequate sunlight reached the ground for the growth of grasses. The system allowed animals and trees to coexist on the same land. East Anglia was a wood-pasture area, and the system was familiar to many of the original settlers of Ipswich; their English experience had much to do with how they used the landscape they found in the New World. Wood-pasture is in some ways the inverse of the coppice system, where the trees are close together and the grass does not grow. In England, late Stone Age agriculturists used the wood-pasture system, and there are even indications that Middle Stone Age hunter-gatherers began to develop the characteristic landscape. By the late Middle Ages, England had evolved three distinct forms of wood-pasture, based roughly on social class. The first was a type of common pasturage, where the domestic animals of a community, whether sheep, goats, or cattle, grazed on publicly owned land; this notion found its way to many New World communities, including Ipswich.

The second form was the park, privately owned land held either by the Crown, by large institutions like monasteries and universities, or by wealthy families and individuals. The chief purpose of parks was to graze not domestic animals but wild ones, chiefly deer. The private owners fenced the parks well, as much to keep poachers out as to keep deer in. The landowners considered deer a crop and harvested by hunting. By the Middle Ages, there were a few more than three thousand parks in England; at about 200 acres each, they covered 2 percent of the land. They had begun to decline in number by the sixteenth century but were still quite abundant and were a familiar sight to the immigrant generation.

A third type of wood-pasture was the forest; purely a royal prerogative, it was introduced into England by William the Conqueror. English usage, from the Middle Ages to the eighteenth century, distinguished quite clearly between a wood and a forest. A wood was an area where trees grew closely enough to exclude most other vegetation. A forest was a legal designation and referred to an area, wooded or not, where the Crown's forest court could levy fines, primarily for the poaching of deer and for the pilfering of wood. Private individuals could own the land. Fines for wood were modest, generally only the value of the item taken, and really allowed the Crown to collect regular payments. A legal forest often covered much more than the wooded portion and was itself a legal thicket. Waltham Forest in Essex was 60,000 acres, of which only 6,000 acres constituted what is now known as Epping Forest. The rest was ordinary farmland and even included a village. Private individuals owned the land itself. The deer belonged to the king, as did the fines for poaching. The commoners, the small landholders, owned the grazing rights and the right to cut for fuel. The large landowners owned the timber and other woodcutting.

Whether common pasture, deer park, or forest, the forms of wood-pasture look similar. Grazing animals eagerly eat the leaves of hardwoods, whether new seedling or leafy branch. Typical of trees growing in a wood-pasture setting is the browse line: any branch or leaf that reaches to within 5 or 6 feet of the ground is summarily nibbled off, leaving the tree with a clean, sharp bottom edge. Young trees need protection for a few years until they are tall enough to branch above the grazing animals, but then they can fend for themselves. In one form of wood-pasture, animals roamed everywhere. In another form, the inhabitants managed wood-growing areas as though they were small coppices of only a few trees and excluded animals by fencing off the wood, leaving other larger areas of grassland and trees to the animals. Trees in wood-pasture also produced timber, and

HEDGEROW OAK

Both English oak and North American white oak prefer to grow as much horizontally as vertically. The hedge divides a road from a field, and the oak is less restrained than its coppice relative: the trunk is shorter and thicker and the branches lower and stouter. English shipwrights looked to oaks such as these to provide curved timber for special use in vessels. From a photograph by the author.

although lack of competition from other trees means that they had an even shorter trunk than a hedgerow tree and no branches on the trunk, they produced timber from the main stem and, if large enough, quite substantial quantities of irregularly shaped timber from the branches.

A coppiced tree cut at ground level was a favorite food of grazing animals. But if a tree was cut 6 to 8 feet or more from the ground, a crop of sprouts grew from the top of the cut trunk. Such trees, called pollards, were quite common in wood-pasture systems. Cut at frequent intervals like coppices, they afforded a convenient way to keep the sprouts out of the reach of grazing animals.

To the English, oak wood had two different forms: sawn and cleft. All sawing of timber in England was done by hand: two sawyers, one standing on top of a log or squared trunk and the other beneath, laboriously coaxed a large, straight saw blade from one end to the other. Every now and then an enterprising investor would set up a sawmill, but the local sawyers would tear it down. The fear, they said (and in this the local lords often supported them), was that a sawmill would put them out of work. It may be, as well, that large parts of England just did not grow enough trees to warrant the investment in a mill.

The technique of cleaving oak preceded the sawing of oak by tens of thousands of years. Rurally, cleft oak was used to make a variety of products that were used locally. Straight-grained, knotless oak logs had strong, unbroken grain and were easy to work. Spokes for wheels, staves for barrels, and rungs for ladders, all needing strength and durability, came from the best trees. Laths, long, thin riven pieces of oak woven between the studs of buildings, supported daub, a mixture of straw, clay, and sand, which sealed the building from the outside weather. And smaller ¹⁄₁₆-inch-thick pieces were woven into crude but durable baskets.

Such was the wood-producing landscape the early-seventeenth-century English settlers of North America left behind: small, highly managed bits of wood-growing land. When people managed tree crops as intensively as they did in England in the seventeenth century, they were really treating trees as though they were a perennial crop, like grass. When a farmer mows or grazes a field, the grass returns the next year of its own accord; when the English felled a coppice, it too returned the next year, and its crop was predictable and regular. Trees are, in a system like this, as much of

POLLARDS

These willows in the Somerset Levels, when young, were cut 8–10 feet from the ground and encouraged, by regular harvesting, to produce new growth in the form of uniformly sized sticks, thereby protecting the new growth from grazing animals, which are fond of shoots. The willow pollards line the sides of a drainage ditch that effectively separates adjacent pastures. From a photograph by the author.

an agricultural crop as any grain or vegetable and require as much attention and wisdom in management.

Oak in New England

Sixteenth- and early-seventeenth-century European reports, like John Smith's, described the New England coast in glowing terms, emphasizing features the English found familiar and comforting. They told of safe harbors, a congenial climate, mile upon mile of fertile, cleared land, and endless forests, some rising right from the ocean, many of them full of oak. The English described what they saw in terms of the agricultural landscape they knew from England, in part because that was the only vocabulary they had and in part because they were attempting to make the New World sound hospitable to investors and to potential settlers. The English visited only in summer and returned before winter came. This short calendar confined their explorations to the immediate coast, and what they saw was limited by season and geography. But the cleared land, with its cover of grasses, promised good crops and ample stores of pasturage and hay for the cereal grain and domesticated animals on which the English agricultural system was built. The coast, with its expanses of grassland, looked as well kept as any English meadow, pasture, or park.

The oaks were a fortuitous presence. The well-stocked forests could provide all the timber resources the English needed to re-create the physical world of England in the new country. No wonder they called it New England. To come across a few thousand miles of ocean and find the same wood—white oak—that built much of the material culture of England was a gift perhaps not sufficiently recognized. The English, with no technological adaptations, made watertight barrels in which to put the stuff they bartered and grew. They made ships to put the barrels in to send to Europe and the West Indies. They made houses in which to live and barns in which to farm. They made the wheels and the carts that moved about the farm. They could make long-lasting sturdy fences. Nowhere else in the future English settlements and in the coming British Empire would they find a natural world that was so like their homeland.

A description of Camden Hills, Maine, by James Rosier, chronicler for George Waymouth's 1605 expedition, is typical:

In this march we passed over very good ground, pleasant and fertile, fit
for pasture, for the space of some three miles, having but little wood,
and that Oke like stands left in our pastures in England, good and great,
fit timber for any use. Some small Birch, Hazle and Brake, which might
in small time with few men be cleansed and made good arable land: but
as it now is will feed cattell of all kindes with fodder enough for Summer and Winter. The soile is blacke, bearing sundry hearbs, grasse, and
strawberries bigger than ours in England. In many places are lowe Thicks
like our Copisses of small yoong wood. And surely it did all resemble a
stately Parke, wherein appeare some old trees with high withered tops,
and high timber trees, masts for ships of 400 tun.[1]

The Ipswich landscape began with the retreat of the last glacier, which
reached its southernmost limit in North America 18,000–20,000 years ago.
The ice that lay 1–2 miles thick over Ipswich gradually melted as the climate grew warmer, and by 11,500 B.C. Massachusetts Bay was free of ice.
Within 1,000 years the first Indians, hunter-gatherers, lived in the treeless tundra conditions of southern New England. Over the millennia, the
climate gradually warmed, and by about 3000 B.C. the forests of eastern
Massachusetts had evolved to their present type, and oak began to grow
in what became Ipswich. Sea level stabilized about 1000 B.C., after the
melted ice returned water to the oceans and the earth's crust rebounded
from the weight of the glacier; at this time Ipswich had its modern to-
pography and flora and fauna.

The first Indian culture to practice agriculture farmed in Ipswich by
700 B.C. By A.D. 1000 the Late Prehistoric culture, whose agricultural prac-
tices would directly affect the landscape the English encountered, was well
established in Ipswich. For more than two millennia the agricultural Indians of the New England coast had carefully formed the landscape that
Thomas Dennis walked. They manipulated the landscape to enhance their
own food supplies, planting crops of corn, beans, and pumpkins on carefully prepared garden plots. The Indians did not have the domesticated
animals of the Europeans—cattle, horses, sheep, goats, pigs, and fowl—but
they intentionally increased the food available to the wild deer by creating great expanses of treeless grasslands and meadow. The forest meets the
meadow at the verge, a narrow strip tens of feet wide where the vegetation of the field rises to the crown of the forest and abundant leafy browse

is at a height deer can reach to eat. Although the Indians had not domesticated deer, they consciously managed them as a crop by providing them with more food than would have grown naturally.

Fire was the Indians' primary tool for controlling the landscape. In the summer, the typical Algonquian group had a village at the coast, where the members grew their crops, fished, and hunted. In the winter, they lived at a village inland. Seventeenth-century English commentators reported that the Indians burned twice a year, in the spring, before the grass came up, and in the fall, before the snows came. The English noted that the burnings added fertility to the soil and kept the countryside "passable" by essentially killing everything but the grasses. The spring burnings, driven by the prevailing, vigorous southwesterly winds, preceded the move of the village to the coast.

After many hundreds of years of such systematic burnings the land of the New England coast looked as stable and cared for as any European landscape. The many bare hills and fertile fields John Smith saw resulted from a deliberate Indian policy of burning, lost in antiquity. By the seventeenth century, the Indians of coastal New England were burning to maintain their cleared lands, not so much to create new open land. The mature, coastal forests of southern New England, primarily composed of leafed, or deciduous, trees with a mixture of evergreen, or nondeciduous, trees, mainly white and red pine, burned only with extreme difficulty. The absence of grasses and small trees on the ground provided little fuel for a fire, and the leafy crown of the woods, beginning 50 feet or more up in the air, was safely out of the reach of flames. Over time, no doubt, some grasslands did return to forest, and some woods were turned to grasslands, but the general appearance of the coast had been stable for centuries by the time the English arrived.

In Massachusetts the English invariably established coastal settlements in the early seventeenth century on the sites of earlier Indian summer villages. The Indians, possessing neither draft animals nor the wheel, had to carry everything by hand. Indian villages combined three important features: they were near the fields where they grew their corn and vegetables; there was good drinking water close by; and wood for fuel did not have to be carried far. Roger Williams, who founded Providence, Rhode Island, in 1636, reported that the Indians, asking why the English had come there from across the ocean, wondered whether it was because the English had used up their firewood and therefore, like the Indians, simply moved to find more fuel. The Indians' firewood often grew in damp, swampy areas, where the fire could not burn. They preferred their firewood on the small side—inches in diameter rather than feet in diameter—since small trees were readily felled with stone axes and were easier to transport than large ones.

The Indians' compact villages—houses, gardens, fields, drinking water, and fuel all close together—were as though made for the English. The coastal Indian groups, nearly exterminated in the early seventeenth century by European diseases, left their settlements for the most part abandoned. It was on such an empty Indian settlement that the *Mayflower* passengers disembarked in 1620, and it was an empty settlement that the immigrants to Boston found in 1630 and that Ipswich took advantage of in 1633.

Oak in Ipswich

The English in Ipswich might have found a landscape created by eons of Indian habit, but they immediately set about defining the land in their own way. From 1634, when written Ipswich records began, until 1709, when the common lands were sold, the town enacted about a hundred regulations and orders pertaining to the harvesting of wood, all duly recorded in the Ipswich Town Records. The first ordinance to do with trees, in November 1634, said that any settler whose house lot happened to contain trees could fell those trees after paying the town a "valuable consideration." This may have been a way of gaining a bit of money for the town treasury, since the usual things on which rates were based—land, dwellings, personal property, and agricultural products—were not yet much in place. The "valuable consideration," then, was a fee for use, much like the fines in the wood-pasture parts of England, and probably represented only the value of the wood taken.

In April 1635 the town ordered that "no man shall sell, lend, give or convey or cause to be conveyed or sent out of this Town any Timber sawen or unsawen, riven or unriven upon pain of forfeiting the same, or the price thereof to the use of the Town."[2] This order clearly states that no timber in any form may be sent from Ipswich. Since all orders after this time are concerned only with common land, it may be that this one is as well and that early in the second year of the town's existence all land was still common, as the divisions into individual lots had not yet begun. In any case, the intent of the order is clear: public resources are not for individual profit. The pressure on the wood resources of coastal Massachusetts Bay communities was intense. First, the towns themselves needed to build their physical world, from housing and barns to fencing. Second, Boston, the largest coastal town, was almost devoid of trees and needed to import almost all its firewood and timber. And third, the growing trade with the West Indies and Europe, upon which much of the economic well-being of the new settlements depended, likewise tended to pull local resources from the coastal forests. The lawyerlike language of this ordinance, and the fact that similar regulations appear in many New England towns in the mid-1630s, may indicate a colonywide concern that towns could lose their timber resources to a growing commerce.

Several times by the middle of the century the town repeated the prohibition against selling wood from the commons. In 1649 the town detailed what forms of white oak were not to leave the town: "any wood, timber, planks, boards, bolts, staves, or caske made of white oak, wch was taken from any of the Townes Comons, under the penalty of 20s. for every tun of timber, wood or caske, and for every 1000 of staves, bolts, planke, or boards, soe transported."[3] Wood meant fencing or firewood, whereas timber meant wood for the frames of buildings and ships and other purposes requiring large pieces of wood. Planks 2 inches thick and up were the standard sheathing for the hulls of ships; boards were thinner—1 inch thick. Bolts were split sections of short logs; staves, cleft from bolts, and casks were the products of the cooper. Commoners could cut wood only for their personal uses. Such stipulations had been made before, but the town was clearly finding it necessary to repeat the old orders with some frequency.

In 1640 the town first mentioned a fine, of ten shillings, for felling trees for sale, again reaffirming the notion that public resources were not for private gain, and for felling without permission of the constable, who represented the town. But apparently the constable was not adequate—perhaps he had favorites, perhaps he was just hard to find, perhaps he felt pressure by certain individuals—and a few years later the town established a committee of four, any three of whom were needed to grant permission.

In any case, timber cutting required official town approval throughout the century.

Beginning in the 1640s, the town shared part of the fine, first giving a third to the official who had to collect it. Perhaps enough infractions went unheeded that the town decided it was worth the payment of a third of the fine to town officials in order to increase the town's share. In 1649, the town also shared the fine with an informant. (What would be the effect if police could keep a share of traffic fines or if one could make some cash by turning in a neighbor?)

By 1642 pipestaves, roughly prepared pieces of white oak used to make large wine casks known as pipes—for which only white oak could be used—became a sort of currency. New England merchants had recently developed a trade with the wine-producing regions of Spain and Portugal for the New World product. In January 1643 the town appointed a committee to over-see the payment of the town's rates to the colony in pipestaves. Six months later, in June 1643, Ipswich for the first time mentioned white oak as the tree species that carried the ten-shilling fine for unapproved cutting; commoners may have been making pipestaves for export from public wood. During the 1640s the town also found it necessary to legislate against the "waste" of wood by the commoners; too much was lying on the ground, rotting. In wood-poor England, the inhabitants had used every last bit of a felled tree; what was not timber for manufacture they burned as fuel, right down to the smallest twigs. They even burned the chips left from hewing timbers and the plane shavings from workshops. But in 1640 the town of Ipswich again legislated that anyone who felled a tree for timber had to cut up the top for firewood within one year of felling; if not, anyone could use it. Perhaps the offenders were carpenters, felling for the frames of houses and barns and cutting more trees than they could use, or perhaps they were husbandmen, needing fencing. In 1649 the town first stated the notion of "fitness": a tree could be used only for "the necessary use of the Towne, in making such ware which only yt sort of timber is fitt for."[4] A large, straight-grained white oak, good enough to make barrel staves, was too valuable for fencing, for which small and crooked trees sufficed. By 1650 Ipswich had established policies regarding the use of the town common land that continued, with some modification, throughout the century: trees from the commons could not be used for individual profit; fines and the means of collecting were established; and white oak received special protection.

During the second half of the seventeenth century the general limitations of the first few decades became more and more specific, and gradually the town with increasing purpose came to control the development of the common lands. It is difficult to say whether the look of the Ipswich landscape in 1700 was something the first settlers in 1634 could have foreseen. But by the middle of the century both local and foreign markets had developed for the town's produce, and the town was becoming prosperous. Economic opportunity attracted newcomers to Ipswich, and many of the children of the immigrant generation chose to stay. The demands for trees for manufacture and building, fencing, and fuel increased. The town adopted policies that attempted to use the tree resources most wisely while at the same time encouraging the development of agricultural land.

In 1650 the town began to limit cutting to certain places. In that year anyone cutting timber in a variety of woods, from Jeffrey's Neck, about 2 miles from town, to the far side of the Chebacco River, more than 4 miles, needed permission from the selectmen. In 1657 the town defined a line 2.5 miles from the meetinghouse, within which strict regulations applied to the felled trees. In 1659 the town moved the line to 3 miles from the meetinghouse, and finally, in 1672, after a brief time at 4.5 miles, it established the line at 3.5 miles from the center of town, where it remained for the rest of the century.

Within these bounds the town sought particularly to regulate firewood. The English habit of using only branches or small trees for fuel proved persistent and required constant correction. The town found it important to regulate lopping, the cutting of branches from standing trees. In 1657 the town allowed lopping of white oak so long as two main branches were left on the tree. Two years later the town completely disallowed the practice but had to repeat the prohibition several times. In 1666 the town required that anyone felling a firewood tree remove the body and brush within two days of cutting the branches. Commoners were cutting trees for fuel but using only the branches and leaving the large trunks and the small brushy ends of branches. At the end of 1669, the town ordered that anyone who felled "timber for posts, rayles, clabord, shingle, wheeles, caske, or building" within 3 miles of the town could take only the trunk—the timber part of the tree—and had to leave for one week all the rest for any commoner to take for firewood.[5] Several months later, early in 1670, the town declared that outside the 3-mile line anyone who felled a timber tree had to cut the tops into firewood immediately and could cut no more firewood until he had carted the tops away. Inside the 3-mile limit, the feller of a timber tree had to leave the tops for one month for any commoner to take. But in 1673 the town said that any commoner who came upon any felled tree in the woods at any time could have the top for firewood, so long as he who felled it was not at work on it.

Besides setting limitations on where trees could be felled "for the fire," the town determined the time of year. Beginning in 1670, it set a two-week period, generally in February, when commoners could fell trees for firewood. In England winter was the traditional time to fell coppices. It was the slack period of the rural calendar, between harvesting and fall plowing and the next spring's planting, and rural people had some spare time. Coincidentally, felling in winter also produced the most vigorous new growth. The stored energy of the trees was still locked in the roots, and the next spring would produce a more vigorous crop of shoots than if the coppice had been felled in the summer, when much of the stored energy had been converted into leaves and new growth, leaving less to produce a new crop of shoots. These reasons pertained in the New World, but there was an additional reason to work in the woods in the winter: snow. In much of England, snow was a rare event and rarely lasted long. But in New England the snows could last all winter and proved to be an advantage for hauling wood from the forests, since it was easier for the draft animals to pull a load on the slippery snow than on bare ground. As a result of this order, then, almost all males who could swing an ax—brothers, uncles, sons, servants—could be seen in the woods at the same time. The town did not intend to limit a household's fuel, but by limiting the time for felling trees for firewood, it made enforcement of the policy easier for the officials and probably encouraged self-policing, since there were now many more potential "informants" in the woods. Additionally, if it was a snowy winter, the presence of many men in the woods helped make trails, a benefit to everyone. The open season was only for firewood; artisans and farmers continued to fell trees for timber or fencing at any time.

Often the most everyday activities were the least likely to have been commented on by contemporaries, unnoted because they did not need to be. Collecting firewood is one of these, and despite the tremendous demands this basic need placed on the resources of the commons, little work has been done on the question of seventeenth-century fuel needs. For the inhabitants of Ipswich, one of the most important household considerations was to determine the family's annual consumption of firewood. The cord, a volume of wood containing 128 cubic feet, has long been the standard unit of measure. Most commonly it was seen as a pile of wood 4 feet high, 4 feet deep, and 8 feet long. Twenty-five cords per year is often cited as the needed amount, but this figure is based on larger eighteenth-century houses. For the smaller houses of seventeenth-century Ipswich, fifteen cords per year per house is probably closer. If the number of commoners in Ipswich in the last decades of the seventeenth century accounted for about two hundred houses, then combined they would have burned about three thousand cords of wood per year—a pile of wood 4 feet wide, 4 feet high, and 4.5 miles long. There may well have been another two hundred dwellings in Ipswich at the time, most of them outside the village, owned outright (many by the sons of commoners) or rented to hired farm help or to journeymen, a steady but constant population in the town.

Forty cords is commonly used as the volume of cordwood on an acre of New England forest. If two hundred houses each burned fifteen cords of firewood a year and there were forty cords on the average forested acre, then each year 75 acres would have been cleared for fuel. If a plot of woodland devoted to growing fuel was left to coppice and could produce another crop in twenty-five years, then about 2,000 acres—3 square miles—of forest grew fuel for the commoners. Double this for the other possible two hundred dwellings in Ipswich, and much of the town's land was devoted to growing fuel.

Because white oak was the most significant tree for manufacture and, along with the hickories, made the best firewood, oak was under particular pressure. The notion of "fitness" excluded white oak as a firewood, but still the tree often needed specific protection. In 1658, the town stated that no white oaks could be cut as firewood; in 1672, it announced a minimum size of 12 inches in diameter at the stump for timber and firewood. Later the same year the minimum size of 12 inches was set for white oak specifically for "studs, rayles and spars."[6] Studs in the period were commonly 3 by 4 inches to 4 by 6 inches, rails were the split horizontals of fences, and spars were pole-sized pieces of wood that went across the rafters of a building to carry a roof of thatch. A carpenter could hew a log not much more than a foot in diameter at the bottom end into a timber 8 by 8 inches to 6 by 10 inches, which quite comfortably provided, when sawn into quarters, four pieces of building timber.

Throughout the century, the town had to weigh the various demands on the common land, encouraging some while discouraging others. As the century went on, some things that had not been problems became problems, like the perceived "waste" of wood. In the first few decades the commonalty may actually have benefited from using only small trees and tops for fuel: the time saved could go toward building the homestead, and cutting more trees than needed for fuel, thereby clearing more land, helped establish agricultural land. But as the population grew, and with it the need for forest resources, problems arose that had not existed in the first few years. Ipswich, like most of the small New England towns, was primarily an agricultural settlement, and wealth was measured mainly in terms of land, animals—cattle, horses, and sheep—and produce.

Toward the middle of the century, the town first used the increasing number of residents as a means of carrying out a policy toward the landscape. In December 1651, the town ordered that "the Surveyors of the Highwayes shall appoint a considerable company of men, to fell the small wood upon the Eastern syde of Jeffryes neck, to prepare it for sowing of hay seed, this to be done before the first of March next coming."[7] This was the first of a series of orders designed to turn woodland into agricultural land. The selectmen appointed the surveyors of the highway annually— in 1651 there were four. They kept an eye on the town's roads and decided where and when maintenance was needed. Every inhabitant of Ipswich over the age of fourteen spent several days a year working on the town's roads, which after only a few decades were still very poor. That the town chose to divert this pool of labor from the roads to create agricultural land indicates that increasing agricultural land was more beneficial to the town. The eastern side of Jeffrey's Neck may never have had good timber on it. However, the fact that the "considerable company" is instructed to fell the "small wood" implies that the site had already been harvested: small wood referred to the shoots that sprout from hardwood stumps. The town would not have focused this public energy on land that could not yield a good crop of hay. The land on Jeffrey's Neck was doomed as woodlot.

Six years later, in 1656, a group of Ipswich farmers petitioned the town for more land to keep their "dry" cattle—either heifers too young to breed or cows between one lactation and the birth of another calf. The inhabitants indicated that the "thick woods, lying beyond the cowe comon is one fitt place for such a use."[8] The town granted the request and appointed a group to determine where the fences would go. The commoners who benefited from the new pasturage were to bear the cost of the fence. The thick woods was presumably suitable for pasturage because, as the word *thick* implies, it was a thicket, a young woods, made of relatively numerous small trees, brush, and possibly brambles, and contained little useful timber. This tract would no longer grow trees. In the thick woods the town accomplished the conversion by cattle (which eat any new growth), not by men with pick axes, shovels, and rakes, as had been the case at Jeffrey's Neck.

The swamps near Ipswich merited their own attention. Some, closest to the village, had probably been sources of firewood for the Indians. Other swamps remained after the surrounding upland had been turned to agricultural land. In 1652 the town instructed the commoners to take their firewood from the swamp between Timber Hill and Brush Hill, each cutting a swath two rods, or 33 feet, wide and taking every tree in his path. The town's intention may have been to drain the swamp, turning it into farmland. Or the town, by felling the trees all at once, may have been turning the swamp into a coppice. The swamp lay conveniently near the village and may have been more valuable for growing wood than as marginal pasturage. Several other times in the 1660s and 1670s the town encouraged the cutting of firewood in the swamps.

Throughout the first three decades of the town's existence, the Ipswich Town Records contain occasional grants to commoners for the felling of trees from the commons. Most of these grants specify white oak, and many of these early grants are to artisans for their trade. But the occurrence of these grants in the records is haphazard. Suddenly, in mid-1666 and continuing for five and one-half years, through the end of 1671, the town records contain a great number: 594 grants of liberty to fell trees were made during this half decade. This proliferation of grants in the Ipswich Town Records was preceded by a lengthy, detailed order passed by the town on February 20, 1666. Among other things the order stipulated that trees could be cut from the Town Commons "only for yr necessary use of building or fencing, or implements of Husbandry, or household stuff."[9] A total of 185 different commoners received these 594 grants, some getting but one or two, others half a dozen or more. In April 1665 a committee appointed to determine the number of rights of commonage had found a total of 203. Almost every eligible right of commonage was exercised at least once during this period. /

The grants are very specific, detailing the number of trees granted, the purpose for which the trees were to be cut, and often the species. A number of grants were for wood for more than one purpose. For instance, in 1668 the wheelwright Isaac Foster was granted "a tree to make pails and measures, and to make wheels for the town's use, and 5 or 6 trees for fencing."[10] There are 794 specific purposes stated for the 594 individual grants.

The detailed grants end abruptly after 1671, and the few later recorded grants are almost all for pine. At the end of the 1660s, Ipswich had finally used all the timber standing on the common lands. The detailed order of 1666 and the numerous detailed grants that followed were probably the town's response to the dwindling supplies: to monitor carefully the distribution of the few remaining resources. Hence, the Ipswich Town Records provide a window of five and a half years into the wood-using habits of the commoners of Ipswich.

About 350 of the 800 stated purposes were for work that would have been done by carpenters. About 100 were for domestic buildings, including 32 houses, and 55 for additions and lean-tos for houses. Many commoners were expanding their domestic space. Sometime between 1636 and 1639, William Merchant, a husbandman, lived in a small, single-room house, the last house on the north side of High Street as one left the village going west. A large, two-story house still stands on that lot, and extensive analysis of its structure indicates that the present building contains Merchant's small, one-room cottage, which, added to several times in the seventeenth and eighteenth centuries, is now but one of several first-floor rooms. Besides houses, carpenters also worked on agricultural buildings and other structures. About 60 grants were for buildings, or parts of buildings used in agriculture, ranging from barns to henhouses. In addition, there were a few grants for bridges and wharves, both things likely made by a professional.

About 200 requests were made to the selectmen by commoners needing trees to make repairs. About half were for shingles, clapboards, and boards, commonly needed items. There were also 42 for sills and 23 for sleepers. Since a grant for a new building or for an addition to an existing building would most likely have included those building parts, the grants were probably for repairs. The ground level of Ipswich buildings—the sills and sleepers—needed much maintenance, not a surprising fact. The number of grants for sleepers, timbers that held a ground-level board floor but themselves lay on the ground, indicates that many of the buildings in Ipswich were without full cellars, which often were under only a part of the first floor. Building members that supported floor boards over a cellar would have been referred to as joists. Again, most of these grants were to the individual commoners, but much of the work that they imply was probably done by professional carpenters.

There were a total of 260 grants for fencing. The large number of requests indicates the vital importance of fencing. The grants vary in their specificity. Some say only fencing; some say only fencing but describe what is to be fenced—a house lot or an orchard, for instance. A number say posts and/or rails; others say posts and/or rails and specify the number of one or the other or both—300 rails and posts for them, for instance; still others specify the number of trees to be felled.

About 150 grants were for artisans besides carpenters or for the work of those artisans. Of this number, 50 were for the work of the wheelwright, more than for the coopers, turners, and joiners combined. It is clear from these grants that the wheelwright also made plows, and most of the grants for agricultural implements were to a wheelwright. Some of the grants do not specify the trade but only the product, like two grants to Thomas Burnham, a carpenter, one for a tree to make drum rims for the Ipswich militia and the other to make pails and measures, straight-sided containers. Artisans other than coopers, like Burnham the carpenter and Foster the wheelwright, made the simpler straight-sided items.

Other grants were for materials needed for some sort of manufacture or product, like several grants for bark for tanning leather and a grant to the Appletons for fuel for malting (the slow drying of sprouted barley), a service they provided to the town's many beer brewers for much of the century. A grant for charcoal went to the blacksmiths to make fuel for their forges. They apparently worked together, since making charcoal was an elaborate and dangerous project, taking several days for a proper, controlled burn. Also included are grants for buildings and equipment used for the making of a product: the fulling, saw-, and cider mills.

By the time Dennis came to Ipswich, town wood and timber supplies were already growing scarce. In 1831, two centuries after the coming of the English, an accounting of Ipswich's roughly 21,000 acres found only 403 acres of "woodlot": the town was not much more than 2 percent wooded. Bound intimately with these changes to the landscape is the joinery of Thomas Dennis. In 1669 when Dennis was granted trees for his trade, the town of Ipswich had been in existence for only thirty-six years. But the trees he looked for, big enough to make his furniture, were a few centuries old and had grown in a forest that was the result of the natural history of the area worked upon by the Indian farmers who preceded the Europeans.

Chapter Three

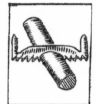

Thomas Dennis in the Woods

ONE CLEAR FALL MORNING in October 1669, Thomas Dennis left his house on County Street, near the meetinghouse in the heart of the village of Ipswich. Now that the crops and hay were in and the fall plowing done, Dennis could turn his full attention to joinery. He needed timber. In the faint, predawn light, Dennis easily found the way behind his house to his joiner's shop. He felt just inside the door for the handle of his ax, which he would use to mark the "6 trees for his trade" that the Ipswich selectmen, at a special meeting the previous February, had granted Dennis, one of sixty-one who received "liberty" to cut from the commons.[1] The town had deemed Dennis's trade to be essential to the community. Other artisans awarded grants in 1669 included coopers, who made barrels, wheelwrights, who made carts and agricultural implements, and turners, who made chairs and spinning wheels; they would be looking, too.

In the woods Dennis needed to be attentive to several different bodies of knowledge. He had to know which standing trees would be best for his purposes, to see into the trees to get the best possible pieces for his furniture; his craft began here with the ability to read the growing trees in the Ipswich landscape. He had to know how to fell and process the trees and how to get them home to his shop; these activities were part of husbandry, the practice of farming in all its aspects. And Dennis needed to know the expectations the town and village placed on his activities. This cultural aspect, rooted in the highly ordered life of the village, required Dennis to know as much about his social world as he did about the world of his craft. What he would make was useful to his fellow townspeople, and the integrity of his craft, carried out in a shop next to his house in the village, was a matter of public knowledge. His neighbors knew his habits— when he arose, how well he stacked his firewood, the sounds of his chopping, planing, and sawing; they recognized his work immediately. And because he was a commoner, Dennis bore further scrutiny from the legal entity of the town and from the selectmen, who administered the town's ordinances.

On the Way to the Woods

Dennis, ax in hand, threaded his way through his dark yard and began the two-and-a-half-mile walk to William Fellows's farm, beyond which lay a remnant of the common forest. In the densely inhabited neighborhood near his house, Dennis barely discerned the jumble of buildings—houses, barns, shops—that made up the waking village. A rooster crowed. In a barn, a cow lowed softly. Someone was splitting kindling. Pigs squealed. Dennis did not notice; all was normal. In the village there were few trees, just the odd shade tree on a street or in a yard and a number of small orchards near houses. In the thirty-five years since its settling, Ipswich had grown from a few houses and barns to a village of more than two hundred homes. Crossing the Ipswich River on the cart bridge near the mills at the Upper Falls, Dennis had a choice: in about a quarter mile, near the end of the village, the road forked. No road went into the forest where he would seek his trees, but both branches of the fork led to roads that were near it. In either case, once he was out of the village, the countryside looked the same, and Dennis could make out, almost as far as the eye could see, acre upon acre and field upon field of cleared farmland. Most of the land was plowed and planted or cut for hay. Some of it consisted of the standard 6-acre planting lots assigned to commoners in the first decade; other parts were the large farms of the wealthy as well as smaller farms put together by some fortunate early comers, husbandmen and tradesmen both, who were able to purchase land. Some of the land was common cropland, used jointly by the commoners, and some was part of the South Commons, where the Ipswich commoners grazed their cattle, horses, and sheep.

Wooden fences consisting of posts and four or five horizontal rails contained the distinct fields; since the domestic animals roamed freely on the common pasture, the fences kept the animals out, not in. The scene looked like the Devon countryside in England that Dennis had left a decade ago, almost all field and pasture and plow land—but for one thing: the fences. In the old country, with its ancient networks of fields, woods, and roads, hedges most commonly divided the fields and excluded the animals; in New England, there had not been time for hedges, and, anyway, there was plenty of wood. Almost all the South Commons fence Thomas passed now had been replaced at least once, and some of it even twice.

From the beginning, Ipswich understood the necessity of fencing. On April 20, 1635, the spring of the second full year of settlement in Ipswich, the town ordered that "all House lotts within the Town are to be fenced by the first of May and such as fail shall pay 2.s pr. rodd beside the payne of doeing it."[2] The first settlers had laid out the principal streets of the village and the house lots by 1635, but the town was still relatively empty. Houses would most likely have been small, the minimum space that would do for the time being, like William Merchant's house. Agricultural shelter was probably minimal; cattle were very expensive in the first years and probably were few. About the houses sprouted the beginnings of vegetable gardens, and some of the rest of the lot may have been planted to grain and corn crops or at least used for hay. Some settlers may even have started orchards in the first years. But implied in the 1635 order is the probability that there were animals about, most likely pigs and cattle, the two basic domestic animals of the first few years in New England.

The meaning of this fencing order is simple: the burden of fencing fell on the person who would suffer loss, not on the person whose animals would offend. Pigs and cattle require two extremes of fencing. Cattle are large and strong, and a relatively tall and strong fence is needed for them. In these first few years the cattle were probably tethered in the house lots or the common pasture, where they could have grazed with no fence to

GEORGE FRANCIS DOW PHOTOGRAPH
OF AN IPSWICH LANDSCAPE, AROUND 1900

The avant-garde Dow took many bucolic photographs of the Ipswich landscape for use by students in an art school he ran in the town during the summer. A young Georgia O'Keeffe studied with Dow. Dow was also friends with those on the North Shore who were rediscovering their colonial past, and his contribution was a thorough and useful eight-volume edition of the Essex County court records and a three-volume edition of the wills and inventories. Courtesy of the Ipswich Historical Society.

contain them. Pigs are small and persistent, and a short, stout fence is needed to exclude them. The presence of both at once, however, meant that both extremes needed to be defended against.

In 1635 the town granted a large lot to the wealthy Daniel Denison. The lot included, in part, "a house lott neere the Mill, containge about two acres, which he hath paled in, and built an house upon it."[3] Pales are vertical pieces of wood fastened to a horizontal rail or rails, which in turn may be fastened to posts. The picket fence is a modern descendant, but the seventeenth-century fences were not made with sawn boards like the picket fence but with split and riven stock. Pale fences show up all over the English New World, from Virginia to Maine. Clearly part of a shared technology, they were the standard village fencing throughout the region. Many of these fences have been reconstructed at living history locations all along the East Coast and have proved an efficient barrier to both pigs and cattle, not to mention sheep and horses, which became more common as the century went on.

Wood for fences can be quite irregular and still do the job; probably the nearest was used first. Fences made by setting the ends of the pales in a shallow trench and nailing or pinning the pales onto one or two horizontal rails themselves fastened to posts about 8 feet apart have proved to be quite sound, proof against rooting pigs below, cattle above, and sheep in the middle. The verticals can be either small saplings split in half or larger trees split and riven into quarters, eighths, sixteenths, or whatever fraction of the log will make suitably stout pieces of wood. Two 4- to 6-inch-wide pales per running foot suffice. The perimeter of Denison's 2-acre house lot was about 1,250 feet; thus, approximately 2,500 pales would have been required to fence his house lot. Fence posts and rails would have needed yet more wood, for a total of eight to ten cords.

With the house lots fenced and the cattle tethered, the nearby planting lots were secure. However, as the number of cattle increased, it became necessary to exclude them from the planting lots. In 1638 the town required the commoners on the north side of the Ipswich River to build a fence almost 2 miles long to contain their common land; those on the south side built one nearly as long. These long common-land fences were intended to protect against cattle and were built with horizontal rails set into posts; pales were not necessary.

The Massachusetts Bay Colony General Court found the local regulation of fencing to be such a widespread problem that it established colonywide standards for sufficiency, which Ipswich in turn had entered into the town records in 1653: "outward fences . . . either genll about any comon field, or pticular about any ppiaty, be it house-lot or planting lot or meddow, be it lesser or greater quantity (except as in the Courts order farmes of 100 acres), and it is hereby ordered, that all the sd. fences, shall be made of pales well nayled or pinned, or of five rayles, well fitted, or of stone walls 3 foote and ½ high at least, or with a good ditch betweene 3 and 4 foote wide, with a good bank and 2 rayles, or a good hedge, or such as is equivalent, upon the banke, all and every one of wch kynds shall be made sufficiently to defend, and keep out Swyne and all sorts of cattle."[4]

The early Ipswich common-field fences were probably of this five-rail sort. A five-rail fence used about two-thirds the material needed for an equivalent length of pale fence, but the material needs were still large. The amount of fencing required in a short time in early Ipswich was great. In its first decade, Ipswich must have consumed on the order of several hundred acres of forest just to supply the first fencing.

Originally the South Commons pastured cattle but since the early 1660s held one of the three flocks of sheep that had become significant in Ipswich agriculture. The South Commons came to be known as the sheepwalks. As he walked, Dennis could see over the low, rolling landscape fragments of the south flock as it grazed. The farmlands near the village were punctuated infrequently by trees. Even the small hills that lay about the village were cleared, most of them by the Indians who had lived and farmed in Ipswich before the English. The occasional tree stood alone in the fields, but trees near the village had become increasingly fewer over the years. Public concern had grown about the lack of shade for livestock near the village. In 1660 the town ordered that no one could fell a tree on any public road or on the commons within half a mile of the village bounds unless there were another tree left standing within 150 feet. The trees closest to town, of course, had been the first to go, cut for fuel. Dennis had to go farther to get suitable trees for his joinery, but trees for firewood, as for fencing, were not so special, and the commoners were using them up rapidly.

So Thomas Dennis had to walk more than 3 miles to find his trees. If wood for joinery were not so demanding, if he just had wanted something for fence posts or rails, there were some trees along the way that would have done, but the trees left near the village would not split as straight as he needed for furniture. For two generations, coopers, wheelwrights, and carpenters had all been after the same large, centuries-old trees Dennis sought; they were needed for staves, rims and spokes, and clapboards and shingles. So Dennis passed William Fellows's and went into the woods by the Mile River, not far from the Hamlet, a small settlement that would become the town of Hamilton, to find oaks that suited him.

Thomas Dennis could never have gone into the woods in England as he did in Ipswich and gotten himself free wood for his joiner's work. In addition, because he could split his stuff out himself, the availability of standing timber on the public lands meant that he could get his material at a lower cost than he could have in England. The oak in all extant Dennis furniture is split and riven from logs. Indeed, only a handful of individual pieces of sawn oak have been identified in all of the remaining seventeenth-century North American joined oak furniture, and there are only a few whole pieces of furniture made entirely from sawn oak. In England, most of the oak in the joined furniture of the period was sawn.

The land near the village looked like England, but as soon as Thomas Dennis entered the Ipswich woods, he was in the New World. The forest was primordial, high, untouched by humans; he had never seen anything like it in England. The sort of trees Dennis looked for are apparent in his furniture. The wood is close grained, often fifteen to twenty annual growth rings per inch but rarely fewer than twelve. Those trees grew close together in old, established forests. Today the second- and third-growth oak common in New England grows in much more open, light-filled woods; modern oak is noteworthy if it contains more than about ten rings per inch. Thomas Dennis's oaks were probably more than two hundred years old on average, and some were considerably older. He could tell much by seeing the trees growing, and Ipswich artisans knew from experience what effects forest type, slope degree and direction, dampness of the ground, soil conditions, and even genetic variation had on local trees. Dennis was looking for large oak, upwards of 2 feet in diameter at chest height, since the panels of his furniture required such size. Anything less than 18 inches in diameter was probably too small to bother with.

Dennis recalled going with his master to collect a few trees his master

FOREST-GROWN NEW ENGLAND WHITE OAKS

These oaks, forced to grow upward by competition with one another, looked nothing like the coppice or hedgerow trees Thomas Dennis knew from England. Tall, thin, straight trunks often did not begin to branch until 30 feet or more from the ground. The first English artisans found that such trees split readily into pieces of wood for manufacture, and Dennis looked for such trees in the Ipswich common land. From a photograph by the author.

had purchased in a nearby coppice. Each winter a section of the coppice was felled, everything cut to the ground. This coppice was rather large, about 100 acres, and was divided into nine parts, one of which was cut each year. The person who felled the wood was responsible for fencing the entire section to keep out domestic animals, which he usually did by weaving small rods between sticks driven into the ground. No one knew how old the coppice was, but it had always been felled and fenced this way. Dennis and his master drove the few miles from Ottery St. Mary in a wagon his master had hired, and they pulled up next to where the woodcutter's oxen had dragged the logs to the road. Dennis and the wagon owner helped his master roll the logs up onto the bed of the wagon. They brought the logs back to the shop, along the ancient road. Dennis helped his master roll them into the shade, near the saw pit, to wait for the itinerant pit sawyers to come by. Every three or four months he had them saw what he needed. Sometimes Dennis would be pitman, pulling down on the saw from underneath, sawdust in his eyes and under his linen shirt.

The first settlers had found that they could easily split New England oak into pieces of wood for manufacture. Oak of all species, on both sides of the Atlantic, is a relatively easy wood to split; but in England, the scattered locations of individual trees meant that not only were the trunks shorter and squatter than in New England but they also contained many more knots and much more twisted grain. Since a split in oak follows the grain, the pieces produced by splitting seventeenth-century English oak would rarely have been straight and true. The habit of growth in New England, on the other hand, generally allowed a split that was straight and free from the influence of knots.

When Dennis entered the woods, he could see the best trees in his mind's eye and, at a distance, could judge straightness of trunk and location of branches. As he got closer, he could estimate diameter and height. Finally, next to the tree, he could see the straightness of bark and any signs of knots, dead branches lying deep in the tree that left subtle signs on the surface. Besides this, there was the usual word among tradesmen about the wood from different parts of town, whether flat or hilly, dry or damp, sand or clay. Some white oak split with a clap in half, leaving two almost perfect pieces, with little to level or plane. Everyone prized this easy-to-work wood, which also happened to plane and shave with little effort, but none more so than the coopers, who shaved and planed all their barrel staves. Some white oak split only with the greatest of effort and left an undulating, curly grain that felt like a washboard and was very difficult to plane or shave. This sort, and other difficult-to-split sorts, were prized by wheelwrights for felloes, the wooden rims of cart wheels, which needed to be tough and to resist splitting. The artisans in Ipswich, like those in all rural communities, would see timber in other artisans' shops or perhaps exchange information at a tavern or after Sunday meeting.

Though far from the village, Dennis was not alone in his search for oaks. The year-old stumps of oaks and unrotted piles of brush from the tops of the trees lay scattered here and there. As the artisans moved necessarily into ever more distant parts of the commons to harvest trees, the qualities of the most recently harvested quickly became general knowledge, and Thomas Dennis might have heard that past Fellows's farm he could expect trees of very slow growth that split easily.

The ground was also uneven: not steeply sloped but rough enough with stumps and large rocks that he decided he'd best get his trees out by sled in the winter, when snow on the ground smoothed the rough forest floor and let the sled slide easily and when the wetter places would be frozen. A cart was out of the question in those woods. When Dennis found a tree he wanted, he marked it with his ax so that Josias Lyndon, his servant, could find it in a few days when he came to the woods to fell the trees for his master.

Little is known about Lyndon, whose designation "servant" commonly denoted either an apprentice or a journeyman. Lyndon was probably a journeyman, since three years later, in the fall of 1672, he found himself in court on a charge of adultery, after his new wife—they were married December 27, 1671—had given birth to a child less than nine months after their marriage. There were those in the community who kept track of such things.

Working in the Woods

Sent by Dennis, Lyndon worked alone and used an ax to fell the trees: felling a tree with a saw required two men. But had Lyndon chopped the trees into logs, he would have lost a foot or more of valuable timber every time he chopped a length. So Lyndon and Dennis returned to the woods with a two-person crosscut saw, known at the time as a "whip" saw, and sawed the oak into short sections, probably from 4 to 6 feet long. Dennis might have left a few longer, in case he needed some larger wood, as he might for doors for buildings, but generally the longest pieces he needed for his furniture were met by the shorter lengths. Dennis and Lyndon, after sawing up the trees, split the short logs into sections called bolts. Most New England artisans, like Dennis, split their bolts out in the woods. Some products, like barrel staves, shingles, and clapboards, and timbers for building, often went from start to finish in the woods. The activities needed few tools and generated a significant amount of waste. In England, the chips and shavings were highly prized as fuel and were gathered up; but in Ipswich, they rotted on the ground of the woods.

Everyone in Ipswich, whether artisan, merchant, minister, or husbandman, had splitting tools. A typical kit included at least one iron wedge and several wooden wedges made from a tough, dry hardwood. To pound them Lyndon used a splitting maul (often called a "beetle"), a large, two-handed mallet with a round wooden head circled on each end with a heavy iron ring, which gave the maul its weight and helped keep the wooden head from disintegrating. The value in a maul lay in the iron rings, which could cost a half day's wages. One set of rings might last generations and survive many new handles and heads.

The bolt, a distinct category of wood, was primarily an artisan's wood, and he could turn it into clapboards, barrel staves, wheel spokes, furniture, or any other product that had to be split from a straight-grained piece of wood. The 4- to 6-foot-long bolt was probably as big as one man could handle in the woods and about the yard and shop; if two men went to do the hauling, the bolts could have been bigger. If they were too small, they would dry out too quickly and become unnecessarily difficult to split and finish. Bolts cut in the fall, like Dennis's, if stored at the shop in the shade away from any breeze, would stay unseasoned and workable until the next fall. He would do the finer splitting and riving at his shop as he needed.

Lyndon examined the first log to split, paying particular attention to the ends. He then went to the top end, placed the small wedge about midway between the heart and the bark, and started it in the end grain of the wood by a few light taps from the back of his felling ax. Lyndon was split-

WHITE OAK RAYS AND END GRAIN

Top, The quartered face of a close-grained piece of white oak; the growth rings intersect this face at 90 degrees. *Bottom,* The end grain. The rays, which show on the end grain as white lines running from the heart to the bark, are the planes along which oak prefers to split. On the quartered face, the rays show as rippling, shiny patches. Drawing by Rex Bradeen.

ting the oak according to a general rule of thumb for all woods: no matter how long the piece or what the diameter, 2 inches or 2 feet, it was always split in half. Therefore, the first split Lyndon made passed through the heart of the tree, leaving two more or less equal halves. If the resistance to the force creating the split is not equal on both sides, the split will run to the lesser side, usually an undesired outcome. An artisan split a half into quarters, the quarters into eighths, and so on.

Lyndon was careful to place the edge parallel to the rays. Rays, easily visible on the newly sawn end grain, run from the outside of the tree to the heart of the tree and carry water in and out; they are planes of natural cleavage, and their large size in oak is one of the factors that make the green wood so easy to split. Often the heart of the tree was off center, so the rays were not true radii, but they did indicate where the log would split. Dennis, as master, might have determined where to saw the trees into short lengths, but choices in splitting were few, limited by what the end of the log indicated about the growth of the tree.

After a few more raps from the back of Lyndon's ax, the small wedge forced into the oak, and the thin edge cut into the wood. Once started, a split shot ahead of the front edge of the wedge, and the work was done by the surfaces of the wedge a half an inch or so behind the edge. The wood fiber was literally cracked apart, not severed by a cutting edge, and the wedge itself could do little to influence the exact route of the split, which wanted to follow the grain—the path of least resistance through the rays. Once the small wedge started the split, Lyndon no longer needed it, and for the rest of the splitting he used large iron or wooden wedges and the maul. He put a larger wedge either into the end grain or into the bark, if the crack had opened wide enough along the length of the bolt. The split encouraged by the second wedge could run the whole length of the log, but chances are it only went part way and then stopped, as the flexible green oak yielded and absorbed the split. But often Lyndon needed only two large wedges to split the bolt from end to end.

Lyndon judged the ease of splitting by how hard he had to strike the wedge with the maul and how far the crack opened. But Dennis, working on a log behind some bushes a few rods away, could tell by the sounds made by the yielding log. If the log contained much interlocked grain, characteristic tearing noises came from the split and could continue for several seconds after the wedge had been struck, as the wood connected to the adjacent faces slowly separated. Wedges often stuck and had to be chopped out with an ax. An advantage of the wooden wedge over an iron one was that Lyndon could safely chop the slivers with an ax or hatchet in the vicinity of a stuck wedge without danger of nicking the ax blade on an iron wedge. A good splitting log would sometimes open up with a distinct pop as a second wedge was driven in and the sides of the crack separated. No tearing noises followed; the faces split cleanly and instantly from each other.

For Lyndon, this first split of the log into two equal halves was the most difficult of all the splits, passing through the twisted juvenile growth on both sides of the heart. But once it was done, he could read the inside of the log for the information it contained. The heart of the tree was not straight, and the wood for several inches on either side of the heart contained vestiges of juvenile branches, apparent as small twigs embedded in the wood when the split happened to pass through or as a slight swelling of the grain when the branch passed nearby. The grain near the outside of the log was straight, but near the heart it undulated to some degree. The first two-hundred-odd years of the tree's life lay open.

Lyndon split the rest of the log. To split the half into quarters he first set the fine wedge on the top end of the half log and started as in splitting the whole log: the wedge lay on a ray running from the bark to the heart. It was somewhat easier to split the halves with the bark of the tree on the ground. Since erratic and interlocked grain is apt to occur near the heart, the half log was more conveniently chopped out if the heart was facing up. Lyndon used the small and large wedges as in the initial split into halves. If the whole log split easily into halves, chances were that the halves would split easily into quarters, unless one of the pieces contained a hidden knot. The quarters, if large enough, became eighths.

Trouble

Thomas Dennis's felling of trees for his trade should have been just another daily event, but this time something may have gone amiss. In April 1671 Thomas Dennis stood in court, accused by Lyndon of cutting eighteen trees, not the six the Ipswich selectmen had granted him. Lyndon had told the court a year before: "Thomas Denis went into the woods and chosed out eighteen trees, and commanded me Josias Lyndon who then was his servant for to falle them and I accordingly did it by his order And the sayde Thomas Denis and I wrought them out into boltes that is to say (16) of them and the other too ly falled in the woodes and are not yet wrought up and thes trees wear falled since the middle of October laste past in Ipswich woods one the south side of the River beyond goodman Fellowes."[5]

In April 1670 the Ipswich selectmen, upon hearing Lyndon's accusation, sent a visiting committee of carpenter Walter Roper, husbandman Edward Chapman, tanner Thomas Hart, and blacksmith Nathaniel Treadwell to the woods to view the disputed trees with Lyndon and Dennis. Roper and Chapman, the carpenter and farmer, knew the common uses of oak as a building and fencing material. Hart, the tanner, understood how oak bark was used in tanning, and Treadwell, the smith, knew about the making of charcoal, which fueled his forge. They all knew about firewood and fence wood. The eyes of these men, with their wide range of experience with the woods and its products, would not miss anything. They knew one another well; they had practiced their trades and farmed together in the town for years. They were Thomas Dennis's neighbors. This was no group of well-off merchants and wealthy landowners, such as dominated the selectmen, but was made up of manual workers who knew between them all that must have been known about the raw materials of the forest. They reported finding eighteen trees felled and agreed that they had been cut the past winter. All but two had been sawn into bolts. Dennis said that not all were his, but Lyndon told Dennis "to his face" that he had worked up all sixteen.

Walter Roper searched the town records and found Dennis's grant under an entry for February 25, 1669, about halfway down a list of sixty-one:

To Caleb Kimball [a wheelwright], to fell for axel trees.
To John Jewett [a farmer?], to fell for a barne.
To Mr. Cobbitt [the minister], for fenceing at his corne lott.
To Robert Lord Jun. [a blacksmith] to repaire his barne.
To Joseph Browne [a turner], to fell for a hovel.
To Goodman Kimball [a wheelwright and father to Caleb], for his trade for the Townes use.
To Mr. Baker [an innkeeper] and Robert Lord [a shoemaker, father of Robert Jr.], to make a Bridge.
To Tho: Dennis [a joiner], 6 trees for his trade.[6]

These commoners had come to a special meeting at which the selectmen approved their requests and the clerk entered them into the town records. Since it was February and the meetinghouse was unheated, the selectmen probably met at one of the ordinaries, either Moses Pengry's, down on the river below Thomas Dennis, or John Baker's, a few houses north of Dennis. (The colony required, for the ease of travelers, that each town have at least one establishment that provided food and lodging, the ordinary.) There the selectmen could conduct the town's business in a room warmed by a fireplace and where the innkeeper's food and drink was at call. There was, no doubt, considerable mingling of the commoners as they waited for their turn to go before the selectmen and discussion of practical matters like the location and condition of logging roads, the species, size, quality, and number of trees, and where to go to find something particular.

Had Dennis cut more than six trees? Disputes between apprentices and journeymen and their masters were common in the seventeenth century. A grudge of some sort could have motivated Lyndon. There is, however, possibly more to the matter. Early in the history of the Massachusetts Bay

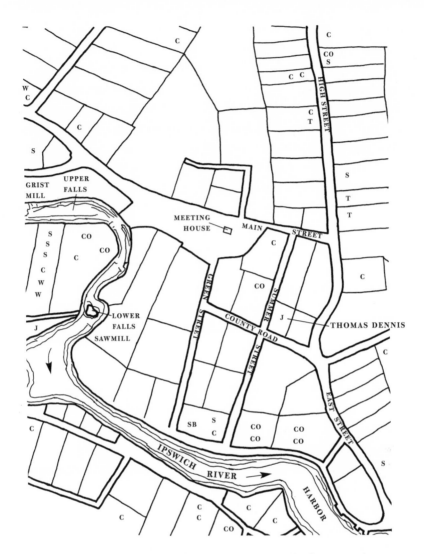

MAP OF
IPSWICH
VILLAGE

This detail of Ipswich places Thomas Dennis's house near the center. Noted are the 43 wood-using artisans (and the allied blacksmiths) who worked in the village during Dennis's residence there, 1667–1706. If other artisans, working mainly in leather and wool, and their seagoing colleagues were added, the map would include more than twice the number of wage earners. The distribution of artisans is fairly uniform throughout town.

The map is based on Thomas Franklin Waters's 1905 reconstruction of the original house lots, laid out in the 1630s. The small, rectangular lots were granted mostly to artisans and the less well off husbandmen. About an acre each and often with less than 100 feet along a town road, they generally remained intact. The larger lots, which went to more well off settlers, were sometimes divided, particularly along the river, where many trades found it useful to set up shop.

Colony, the General Court decided that all violations of local ordinances less than twenty shillings could be dealt with by town officials. The handling of these "small causes" at the town level was intended to keep the colony courts from clogging with many minor cases. By the time Dennis committed his alleged offense, the fine in Ipswich for felling a tree without town permission was twenty shillings. The colony towns apparently got around the maximum fine set by the General Court by considering each individual tree to be a specific instance.

Ipswich adhered to the colonywide practice of giving half of the fine to the accuser, and Lyndon stood to earn a substantial fee if he turned Dennis in. In May 1670 the town charged Dennis with illegally cutting ten trees more than the six he had been allotted: the two that had yet to be cut up into bolts may not have counted against Dennis. The town reduced Dennis's fine per tree from the twenty shillings per tree to ten per tree, probably because Dennis was settling separately with Lyndon, and then further reduced the number of illegal trees to five, for a total fine of fifty shillings. Lyndon's half of Dennis's fine remained ten shillings each for the ten trees Dennis had cut improperly, or one hundred shillings. In March 1671 Lyndon attempted to cash a bond from Dennis in the amount of five pounds—one hundred shillings.

Lyndon first tried to get his payment from Dennis, who refused. Dennis sent Lyndon to Francis Wainwright, a well-to-do merchant down the street, to have the bond cashed. There was little hard currency in New England, and merchants often served as small bankers. Wainwright, from his stock of goods, could give payment to Lyndon, and Dennis would repay Wainwright. When Lyndon first went to Wainwright, the journeyman said he wanted to be paid in penistone, an imported fabric worth about three shillings per yard. Wainwright had none in stock but said it could be on the next bark (a three-masted vessel) from Boston. According to William Cogswell, a well-to-do farmer who happened to be at Wainwright's at the time, the merchant also offered Lyndon fifty shillings in goods and fifty shillings in pine boards, an offer that Lyndon refused. Lyndon may have felt that the fabric, 35 yards of which he could have carried in a single armful, was a more convenient way to receive his payment than was fifty shillings' worth of pine boards, which, at the common price of forty shillings per 1,000 board feet, could have weighed upwards of a ton. The debt, in any event, appears to have been paid.

Dennis's case should have stayed at the local level, as was the usual practice for infractions of community ordinances. It made its way to the court not because Dennis cut the trees but because he was alleged to have lied about the matter. A lie was too serious a matter for local action and, according to the laws of Massachusetts Bay, was to be dealt with by the courts, not the towns. The case dragged on for more than a year. In May 1671 the town instructed Mr. Paine, an Ipswich attorney, to get the fifty-shilling fine from the nonpaying Dennis. The town had already "distrained" the estate of Thomas Dennis, physically removing property of his equal to the amount of the fine. When Dennis paid his fine, he would get back the cow and pine boards that Robert Lord, the marshal, a paid official who conducted much of the town's business, had taken from Dennis. Grace, Dennis's wife, apparently became quite angry, and a year later the town fined Grace for "affronting" Robert Lord when he came to attach her husband's estate.

The case finally ended in 1672, when Thomas Dennis said publicly, in court, that he had wronged the Ipswich selectmen. The selectmen, in turn, forgave him and canceled the fine.

Chapter Four

The Town at Work

APPROACHING IPSWICH from the west in the latter part of the seventeenth century, coming on the road from Rowley and Newbury beyond, one passed through an orderly agricultural landscape. At this end of town, just behind the backyards of the houses, lay some common fields. The Rowley road was called West End where it entered the village; about a dozen houses lay along the street. At first one saw the peaks of roofs, chimneys, and puffs of wood smoke. On coming closer, the fences became clear. The inhabitants included two shoemakers, two wheelwrights, one carpenter, one brickmaker, and several husbandmen. In front of every house and separating all the house lots, endless ribbons of weathered brown pickets, close enough together to keep out chickens and piglets, fenced in the yards. Almost everything, in fact, was some shade of brown—the unpainted fences, clapboards on the houses, shingles on the roofs, plain boarding on the outbuildings; the roads, house yards and barnyards, the few shade trees in winter, all brown. Otherwise, depending on the time of year, green or white alternated, but in any season the village itself wore mostly brown. A few well-to-do folks had the painter pick out a house's trim in a bright vermillion, but that bit of carefully chosen ostentation did little to change the overwhelming brown of the village. The white, clapboarded New England village was almost two centuries away.

The town Thomas Dennis knew had already defined itself economically. Its rich farmlands allowed a market agriculture, primarily in cattle, to develop in the town's first decade. Only a few years after the town's founding, Ipswich beef won a reputation for quality and reliable supply and found a ready market in the new and growing Boston. The demand for beef and the resulting hides in turn encouraged significant local manufactures in leather processing and leather products, like shoes. There was more work for coopers, already busy making casks for Ipswich's fish. By the 1650s the raising of sheep for wool and the production of wool cloth had become common in town, as it was in the region of England from which many of the early immigrants had come. But the richness of Ipswich's farmlands might have been less exploited had not a significant number of East Anglian immigrants of means, many with mercantile interests, settled in the town. This group of immigrants adopted an aggressive policy of trade and export, as their class had done in England; as early as 1641 the town formed a committee of prominent men "for furthering Trade." Among other things committed to their care were "putting up Bouys, [and] Beacons" to aid shipping.[1] They were a practical lot.

Because oceangoing ships of even modest size could not reach the town's harbor, Ipswich never became a major port. Still, a number of seagoing residents either lived in the town or serviced the harbor; there were fishermen, who were often financed by local merchants, and ship owners (like Dennis's next door neighbor Robert Dutch), who hired out their services. The most convenient port for several inland towns, Ipswich became a market town and supported several merchant families. During all of the seventeenth century and much of the eighteenth, Ipswich ranked only behind Boston in the amount of colony taxes it paid, one measure of the wealth of its townspeople.

Ipswich supported numerous artisans, some of whom serviced the local population, like the carpenters whose work mostly lay close to home, and some of whom produced largely for export, like the many shoemakers and glove makers. Artisans who worked with wood were by far the most numerous, about 90 in the last four decades of the seventeenth century.

Carpenters came with the first settlers—there was at least one, Thomas Howlett, among the dozen who wintered the first year—and numbered almost 50. Besides carpenters, there were in the forty-year period 12 coopers, 7 wheelwrights, 7 turners, 6 ship carpenters, and only 2 joiners before the 1690s, when 7 more appeared. The number of carpenters exceeded that of all the other wood-using trades together. Most of the ship carpenters lived and worked in Chebacco, which started to become a shipbuilding center toward the end of the century; only Moses Pengry's shipyard operated in the village of Ipswich.

Those in the masonry trades, about 7, mainly masons and brickmakers, worked closely with the carpenters. Eleven blacksmiths supported the wood-using tradesmen and also did iron work for the farmers. Twenty-five artisans worked in some way with the by-products of cattle—butchers, soap makers, tanners, curriers, shoemakers, glovers—and 24 worked in fiber, in particular wool—weavers, fullers, dyers, tailors, and felt makers. These 70 or so artisans were professionals. Like the 90 wood-using artisans, most of them probably had a regular series of apprentices, and many employed a journeyman or two. The total number of artisans working in all the trades could have been about 250–300, about a quarter of the town's male population. In addition to these artisans, at least 16 went to sea, as fishermen and ship owners. For the most part these skilled workers were only of average wealth. Most of the rest of Ipswich's inhabitants were husbandmen, and most, like the artisans, were of middling wealth.

Ipswich also had a small group of elite, from well-to-do farming or merchant families in England. Several were graduates of Cambridge University. About a dozen and a half had land grants of several hundred acres. Besides the wealthy farmers and merchants there were ministers and physicians and several who would become political, military, or spiritual leaders of the Bay Colony; indeed, Ipswich was a leading intellectual center of New England.

Many of the elite had capital to invest. Some of these men have already had their stories told: because they often played a part in consequential events and because they were often given to writing down their thoughts, they have provided both reason and fertile ground for generations of historians. The artisans, however, rarely played a role in significant events or, if they did, were bit players and almost never wrote down their thoughts.

They come alive only as chance mentions in seventeenth-century documents, usually short mentions at that, and none of them is sufficiently well documented to provide a reasonably complete sense of what his vocational life was like. But when these artisans are taken as a whole, a picture emerges of a typical sort of artisan, and many of the generalizations to be drawn from this group as a whole can apply to Thomas Dennis, himself an average sort of artisan.

Carpenters

Everywhere one looked in Ipswich during the century, one saw carpenters at work. Carpenters made buildings by joining large timbers together intricately with mortise and tenon joints; their work also included exterior coverings, floors, and doors and windows. Carpenters, the most numerous of the artisans, were concerned in the 1630s and 1640s with building dwellings and agricultural buildings for the new settlers. By the middle of the century, as immigration slowed, some new work continued as the town gradually grew, but repairs and additions to existing buildings, in part made possible by the economic well-being of the town as a whole, kept the carpenters busy and their demands on timber supplies constant.

For the frames of their buildings they almost invariably used white oak, one of the many demands for that species. They preferred trees that were small to medium in size. Since carpenters hewed the principal framing timbers of a building from the log, a rather laborious and time-consuming process, they chose the smallest possible tree that contained the square- or rectangular-shaped timber they needed. A 12-foot post, 8 inches square, for instance, needed a log only about 11 inches in diameter at the top end. Such a tree, grown in a thick forest, might have been less than about 16 inches in diameter a few feet off the ground, not a very large white oak. Trees for frames did not have to be particularly good. Crooked trunks, irregular grain, knots, and twist, all negative characteristics for trees to be riven, like those the coopers and joiners sought, made little difference to the carpenter.

Carpenters also used many smaller pieces of oak in timber frames—numerous joists, studs, and common rafters—which ranged from 3 by 4 inches to 4 by 6 inches. In the earliest days the carpenters themselves

COMENIUS CARPENTER

An engraving, done in 1658, from the first illustrated book for children, *Orbis sensualium pictus* (The physical world in pictures), by Johann Amos Comenius, a Moravian cleric and educator. Each of the more than 150 single-subject engravings is accompanied by a Latin text, keyed to the numbers on the engraving. In the English translation the Latin text is paralleled by an English version. The seventeenth-century English text reads: "We have seen Man's food and clothing: now his Dwelling followeth. At first they dwelt in *Caves*, 1. then in *Booths* or *Huts*, 2. and then again in *Tents*, 3. at the last in *Houses*. The *Woodman* felleth and heweth down *Trees*, 5. with an *Ax*, 4. the *Boughs*, 6. remaining. He cleaveth *Knotty Wood* with a *Wedge*, 7. which he forceth in with a *Beetle*, 8. and maketh *Wood-stacks*, 9. The *Carpenter* squareth *Timber* with a *Chip-Ax*, 10. whence *Chips*, 11. fall, and saweth it with a *Saw*, 12. where the *Saw-dust*, 13. falleth down. Afterwards he lifteth the *Beam* upon *Tressels*, 14. by the help of a *Pully*, 15. fasteneth it with *Cramp-irons*, 16. and marketh it out with a *Line*, 17. Thus he frameth the *Walls* together, 18. And fasteneth the great pieces with *Pins*, 19."

would saw this wood with a pit saw from trees they had already hewn square or rectangular. One man stood on top of the log and the other underneath, and they together forced the long saw blade through the wood. The man on top pulled the saw up during the return stroke, and the man underneath pulled the saw down on the cutting stroke. The work was slow and dusty: it took about fifteen minutes to saw by hand an 8-inch-wide board 12 feet long. In 1649 merchant Jonathan Wade obtained from Ipswich the right to set up a sawmill on a site he found suitable, and he built his mill in well-forested Chebacco. Not until 1665, when the town granted Wade the right to put up another mill at the falls in Ipswich, could carpenters have lumber sawn in Ipswich village.

Besides oak for the frames of buildings, carpenters needed pine trees sawn into boards to sheathe the walls and often the roof, for flooring, and for most of the interior finishing—paneling, doors, shelving, and so on. These boards were sawn by water-powered sawmills. Although England relied exclusively on the pit sawyer for boards, in the New World entrepreneurs immediately set up sawmills. In the 1630s a number were built in the Piscatiqua region near Portsmouth, New Hampshire, where vast pine forests of large trees grew. Most of the lumber was shipped to the coastal towns of the colony. Shingles covered the roofs; shingles or clapboards, the exterior walls of most New England buildings. Locally, carpenters rived shingles and clapboards from the log, and the trees for such products needed to be of a high quality, straight grained and free of knots. They had several species from which to choose: white oak, Atlantic white cedar, and red and white pine.

Walter Roper, the carpenter who served as tree watcher and looked up Thomas Dennis's grant in the town book, lived in the West End. Roper, who first appeared in Ipswich records about 1650, served many times as one of the appointed town officials who carried out town policy on common-land trees. His title, Goodman, indicated the esteem in which the town held him. The town frequently allowed Roper to cut trees on the commons. In 1671 he felled enough for one hundred fence rails and the required posts and a few months later cut enough white oak trees to build a barn. Roper, like his fellow Ipswich artisans, practiced at least some farming. And, like the other carpenters, he did a variety of work. He built and repaired houses and laid shingles. He replaced sills in the house of John Spark, the innkeeper, whose son had married Roper's daughter. In 1670 the town granted Roper twelve trees to make looms and loom tackle; depending on the size of the trees, he could have made many looms that year for the increasing number of commercial weavers.

The trusted Roper also made frequent appearances as a witness in court cases. Nonetheless, in 1666 he cut trees from the commons without permission, and the selectmen summarily requested his attendance at their next meeting. Cutting trees against order, though frowned upon, was not heinous, and during the century the town fined about 150 commoners, a total that does not include the many whose fines probably went unrecorded. Roper died at the age of sixty-nine in 1680, worth almost two hundred pounds, a reasonable estate for an artisan. His son, Nathaniel, inherited half of his five pounds' worth of carpenter's tools.

The large and active Burnham family did well in New England. Thomas Sr. came to Ipswich in the early 1640s. He eventually owned about 140 acres of land, at least 30 of which the town granted to him. This larger-than-average grant of land indicates that he came to the New World with some means and social status. Like Thomas Howlett, another Ipswich carpenter and one of the original twelve settlers of Ipswich, who eventually owned about 100 acres, Burnham probably added to his holdings by actively buying and selling. In Ipswich only individuals of substantial financial worth became selectmen. Burnham became one in 1653, one of the few artisans to be a selectman. Before that the town had a number of times appointed him a surveyor, responsible for laying out grants from the commons. In 1657 the town requested that he keep order in the meetinghouse during Sunday services, "that youth be not unruly."[2]

In 1651 and 1670 the town granted Burnham white oaks to make pails and measures. If only these references to him existed, it would seem that he was a cooper. Liquid-tight barrels, with their curved staves, were among the most difficult wooden objects to make; but straight-sided containers like pails were rather simple. It is likely that Burnham filled spare time with the manufacture of this product, which the town valued enough that it allowed the use of public wood. Thomas Sr. also received about a dozen other grants from the town, like the one in 1669 for 300 or 400 fence rails and the required posts; by this time he could have been replacing old fence. In 1660 the town hired Burnham to complete the town wharf, which, like the roads, was built by labor the town required from its male inhabitants. The town dismissed those who chose to help on the wharf from their obligation to do road work. The town also paid Thomas Sr. for work on the county bridge in 1683 and on the schoolhouse in 1690.

In 1667 Thomas built a sawmill in Chebacco, the first the town permitted there after Jonathan Wade's 1649 sawmill. The town did not give such grants lightly. There had to be a need, and the individual given the grant had to have the financial means to build and maintain the mill. Grants for mill sites in particular amounted to a monopoly, and in return the town expected good quality. Wade was a wealthy merchant, as were the grantees of most of the other grist- and fulling mills in seventeenth-century Ipswich. They belonged to a class, it would seem likely, that would not have done any physical work on the mill but hired it all out, both the making and the running. The carpenter Burnham, however, probably built his own mill and did the sawing himself. In 1668 he received a grant for materials for a pair of great wheels, likely a part of the equipment needed for his sawmill. At least about 8 feet in diameter, the axle of the great wheels stood about 4 feet off the ground. The heavy, butt end of the log to be moved was raised up to the underside of the axle. Draft animals pulled the great wheels, the top end of the log dragging along the ground.

Thomas had at least two sons who practiced carpentry: Thomas Jr., who is mentioned in the records of the 1670s and 1680s, and Moses, who shows up but twice and may have moved. Thomas Burnham Jr. was also a commoner, for in 1671 he received a grant to fell for a house 20 feet square. Rarely were a father and son both commoners at the same time, since the right went with the house lot, and the son usually had to wait to inherit his father's house. The Burnhams apparently had enough family money that both father and son, at the same time, were able to afford the privilege. Thomas Jr. in 1668 worked shingling the meetinghouse roof with three other carpenters, Walter Roper, Ezekiel Woodward, and Elihu Wardell. In the early 1680s the town paid him twice for work on the meetinghouse, once for work on the schoolhouse, and once for mending the bell wheel in the meetinghouse, a frequently repaired object, according to the number of payments for its repair. The town also paid him for serving two warrants.

Thomas Sr.'s brother, John, had immigrated a few years before Thomas.

John may also have been a carpenter. In 1674, his son, John Jr., "carpenter," a half owner along with Abraham Perkins, another carpenter, of a new ketch (a small, two-masted vessel) of 30 tons, disputed the capacity of the ship, thinking it smaller. Two decades later, in the early 1690s, John Jr. built two dams and gristmills in Chebacco. The town ordered the first dam moved, since it apparently endangered woodland, by this time a valuable resource. With land growing scarce, investing in shipping and mills afforded a way for those of sufficient means to increase their capital. In 1696 the town granted yet another Burnham, James, a small amount of land for a malt kiln, another commercial endeavor regulated by the town.

The Storys, like the Burnhams, were carpenter/entrepreneurs. In 1645 William Story, a carpenter, turned himself in for cutting white oak trees in the Chebacco common lands, for which the town fined him two shillings, about two-thirds of a day's wages. For most of the seventeenth century an apprenticed artisan's wage was three shillings per day. But Story, like Walter Roper, was known by the reverential title Goodman, and, as with Roper, the town occasionally called him for public service. The town paid him for some work at the Watch House in 1648 and, in 1683, for a coffin. In 1668 the town granted Story liberty to fell white oaks for timbers for a house frame and others for a lean-to addition, both projects for other commoners. In 1671 William Story requested and received liberty to set up a grain and fulling mill in Chebacco, and a year later he obtained town approval for a dam, most likely for the mill.

Since the town had already permitted Thomas Burnham Sr. to build a sawmill in Chebacco in 1667, it granted William Story what was needed next, the grist- and fulling mill. A son, Seth, born in 1646 and also a carpenter, later in the century became part owner of a sawmill in Chebacco. Seth, like some other sons of well-to-do artisans, early in his career was able to purchase a house lot with commonage, for in the 1660s he received a number of grants for trees, for a barn floor and sills, for a sheephouse, and for nine hundred fence rails and the necessary posts. There was at least one other son: in 1668 William Story, William Jr., and Seth were in a dispute with the town over whether thatch they had cut came from private or public land. John Kendrick, a cooper in Ipswich village, was loading barrel staves in Chebacco when he saw the Storys fill three canoes with thatch. These canoes were most likely cut out of a single pine log, in the Indian fashion. To carpenters who specialized in large, two-handed edge tools like broad axes and adzes, such canoes would have been easy to make. "Thatch" usually referred to grass that could not be fed to animals; closely woven and overlaid, it went onto barn and outbuilding roofs or became bedding for cattle.

In 1673 the town ordered the elder Story to take the son of John Leeds as an apprentice. Leeds apparently died in financial straits, and several times the town paid for services for Goodwife Leeds, his widow. Towns occasionally tended to the well-being of minor children by placing them in apprenticeships, seeing it as in the best interest of both parties: the child would grow up learning a trade, and the town would be spared the burden of dealing with another indigent. In this case it was most likely that the town did not force Story into the arrangement, since an unwanted affiliation would do neither any good. The town instructed Story "to teach him his trade, also to read and write and give him a set of tools when his time is out."[3] Story, the master, was sixty-two years old; he would be sixty-nine when the apprenticeship ended, if the lad was fourteen years old when this agreement was made and the time period was the typical seven years. Story must have been actively practicing his trade in order to have taken on this community responsibility, but, since the unfinished time of an apprentice often passed on to the heirs, one of his sons may have benefited from the arrangement.

George Norton, a carpenter, immigrated to Salem in 1639. By 1642 he lived in Ipswich, for in that year, along with four others, he laid out the boundary between Ipswich and neighboring towns Gloucester and Manchester, a task begun near the meetinghouse at a white oak marked on four sides and accomplished with a compass. In 1652 and 1653 the town contracted with him for work on the meetinghouse. He died in Salem in 1659, and his inventory, which indicated that his eldest son, Freegrace, one of ten children, was twenty-four at the time, included "sawes, boarers, axes with other tooles, 2li. 18s. 6." The total value of George Norton's estate was £136.11.06 and included—in addition to the usual household goods, corn, wheat, barley, hay, apples—a mare and two colts, numerous pigs, six oxen, four cows, and eight young cattle.[4]

Freegrace was a carpenter of many abilities. In 1667 the town allowed him to fell timber for a house, presumably his own. Also in that year the town hired him and Ezekiel Woodward to hew timbers for the meeting-house roof; and in 1670 the same two carpenters built galleries in the meetinghouse. In 1671 the town gave Freegrace two separate grants, one for "coggs, and rounds, and starts for the mill"—frequently replaced parts of the gearing—and the other for "3 trees for joynary worke for Town's use."[5] Besides general carpentry work, Freegrace could do the work of the joiner and the work of the millwright, which would seem in the period to have been often a specialty rather than a distinct trade. The carpenter Elihu Wardell, for instance, built a fulling mill for Richard Saltonstall in 1674. With the spare parts, Freegrace could repair the gristmill in the center of the town. Richard Saltonstall, one of the town's wealthiest inhabitants, had held the right to the gristmill since 1635. Saltonstall, the son of a landed English family (his father was Sir Richard), was mostly an absentee landlord. He spent much of his time either in England or in his other New World holdings.

In 1674 Freegrace Norton, then in his late thirties, operated the gristmill. In May of that year he was fined forty shillings for "falsehood or extreme neglegence" in his milling, and the court required him to keep a scale ready at all times for weighing grist, the grain to be ground, and to be generally in attendance at the mill.[6] John Spark, who operated an ordinary near the meetinghouse and appears to have done much baking, complained of the quality and quantity of the grain he had Norton mill. Spark had found that his grist was also sometimes short when Thomas Waite, also a carpenter, had been miller. (A carpenter's ability to repair a mill apparently qualified him to be a miller.) Spark complained to Richard Saltonstall, who promised to correct matters, but nothing happened, so Spark brought his wheat to Rowley, the next town, to be ground. He discovered that he lost the same amount of measure at Rowley as he had at Ipswich and attributed the problem to the wetness of the previous growing season. He added that although he often missed measure in years past he did not feel that Norton himself was stealing his grain but that the mill was poorly secured against theft and that anyone could steal from grain waiting to be ground.

Moses Pengry, who also had an ordinary, on the river down the hill from Thomas Dennis's, reported that he had been at the mill one day when the wheat wheel was grinding. Pengry brought corn to grind on the Indian mill, and while he waited, he saw Norton take an empty bag and put about half a bushel of the wheat meal into it, put it under his arm, go into his house, and return quickly without it. In all, twelve people testified against Norton, including Thomas and James Burnham and Nathaniel Lord, all carpenters, Caleb Kimball, a wheelwright, and Josiah Clarke, a cooper. Clarke further reported that he had gone to the mill to have corn ground and that Norton said he would put a peck of rye in his corn grist this time, and a half peck next time, in exchange for a pint of brandy. Clarke returned quickly with the brandy. Another customer had come to have rye ground. Norton told Clarke to wait, and Clarke watched Norton remove rye from the man's grain while his back was turned and scoop it into Clarke's grist.

In October 1675 an Indian bullet killed Freegrace Norton, a sergeant in the militia, at Hatfield on the Connecticut River in the central part of the colony. The next spring Francis Wainwright, a wealthy merchant and executor of the estate, found that Norton's assets fell short of his debts. When he left for war, Norton had been at work making repairs to a house belonging to Dr. Philemon Dane, the physician. Four carpenters—Thomas Burnham, Walter Roper, Abraham Tilton, and Elihu Wardell—appraised the value of the work Norton had completed before he put his tools down and left suddenly. Artisans could judge the work of artisans better than anyone else. They found that he had framed and laid two pine floors, hung two doors, laid a stone cellar and a thousand bricks, made two pairs of stairs, whitewashed a room, and installed glass, for a total value of £24.12.06, almost a third of his entire estate. The carpenter Freegrace did the work of a mason, a painter, and a glazier, besides having done joinery and millwrighting and having been a crooked miller.

Coopers

About ten coopers made barrels in Ipswich during the latter part of the seventeenth century, about five or six of them working at any time. This large number of artisans practicing a very precise and limited craft says much about Ipswich at the time: coopers were the packaging industry, and Ipswich, with its rich agricultural land and fishing industry, had much to package. The cooper was a true specialist; he did nothing but make casks. (The barrel was a certain size of cask and in the seventeenth century had a precise meaning, not a general meaning as it does now.) Two distinct sorts of cask predominated, those made for dry goods, which the cooper found simpler to make, and those meant to hold liquid, which required near-perfect workmanship and materials. Only white oak could be used for watertight casks, since only that species of oak possessed the required strength and flexibility, as well as a watertight grain. Red oak, which had long, open pores and soaked up liquid like a wick, found use in dry casks.

A coopered cask was a deceptively simple-looking object. Narrow and relatively thin strips of wood, never more than a few inches wide, made up the sides of a cask. A cask, by definition, swelled in the middle and narrowed at each end. Each stave had a similar shape, tapering from a maximum width in the middle of its length to a lesser width at each end. The cooper made the joint between neighboring staves by carefully planing the edges of the staves to a precise and flat bevel, accurately enough that there was as tight a fit as possible between the two edges. The cooper made this tapered angle by that ancient measuring tool, the eye. He learned during apprenticeship just how to hold the stave as he planed its edge. He needed to do other things by eye: taper the width of the stave just the correct degree with an ax, and know how many staves of what size and taper each different size of cask required. Correctly learned habit and practice were the hallmarks of the cooper's training, and the proof of the work was in the result: a cask of precise capacity that did not leak.

In 1641 the colony regulated the manufacture of casks for "any Liquor, Fish, Beef, Pork or any other Commodities to be put to Sale" and required that casks be made to the "London Assize," the standards adopted by the City of London.[7] Each size cask required a different set of formulas. The cooper whose casks did not contain the legally required volume was fined. So important was the expectation of full and fair measure in matters of trade that the colony also created two related positions. The gauger of cask, found in towns where produce was packed for export, measured each completed cask. He signified his approval by branding the cask with his distinct mark. (Each cooper, for his part, had a unique brand with which he, too, marked his casks.) The packer, also found in exporting towns, did not measure capacity but saw to it that the contents were well packed, "that is to say, Beef and Pork, the whole, half or quarter, and so proportionately, that the best be not left out. And so Fish, that they be packed all of one kinde."[8] These decrees regulating the size and packing of casks attempted

COMENIUS COOPERS

An engraving from Johann Amos Comenius's *Orbis sensualium pictus*
(1658). Here is the seventeenth-century English text: "The C*ooper*, 1.
Having an *Apron*, tied about him, maketh *Hoops* of *Hazel-rods*, 3. Upon
a *cutting-block*, 4. With a *Spoke-Shave*, 5. and *Lags*, 6. Of *Timber*, Of
Lags he maketh *Hogsheads*, 7. And *Pipes*, 8. with two *Heads;* and *Tubs*,
9. *Soes*, 10. *Flaskets*, 11. *Buckets*, 12. with one Bottom. Then he bindeth
them with *Hoops*, 13. Which he tyeth fast with small *Twigs*, 15. By means
of a *Cramp-Iron*, 14. and he fitteth them on with a *Mallet*, 16. And a
Driver, 17."

to establish in the early years a standard and dependable unit of trade, whether the destination was the wood-poor city of Boston or the West Indies. Since most sorts of trade required casks, whether within the colony or foreign, the cooper accompanied the farmer and fisherman. Indeed, so central was the cooper to the well-being of a new settlement that coopers were among the first to settle a new town.

In 1646 colony officials, worried that Massachusetts was sending inferior pipestaves to Spain and Portugal, where they were made into long, thin wine casks called pipes, and that the market might be lost, issued regulations for pipestaves. In every town that exported staves, a "Viewer" of pipestaves was to examine each stave and reject those that had worm holes, a frequent complaint, and all those that did not meet minimum size: 4½ feet long, 3½ inches wide, and ¾ inch thick. The staves were to be hewed, with a hatchet, to within ⅛ inch of those dimensions, a tribute to the skill with which a practiced worker could use that seemingly clumsy tool.[9]

The career of cooper Thomas Boardman Sr. followed the careers of the more fortunate of the carpenters. He came early, accumulated land, and, when he died in 1672, had an estate worth £553.06.6, much higher than that of the average artisan; about £350 of his wealth was in land and buildings. Included in Boardman's estate were £5 worth of cooper's tools. When Walter Roper died, his carpenter's tools were worth the same, £5, which sum might have been a standard amount for the working tools of a fully equipped artisan. Both men, although elderly, seem to have been working at their trades in their later years. In 1692 the town granted Boardman's son, also Thomas, liberty to set up a gristmill on Labor in Vain Creek, partway between Ipswich and Chebacco. The Boardmans, like the Burnhams and Storys, were artisans turned entrepreneurs.

In 1643 the cooper William Douglas, a commoner in 1641, felled trees without permission, and the town routinely fined him. In 1653 the town granted him white oaks "for the Towns use," the usual formula.[10] In 1670 he again felled trees illegally, and this time the town took away his right of commonage for two years. In 1652 Douglas bought a part of a house lot adjacent to the property of the carpenter Theophilus Wilson, whose son, Sherborne, apprenticed with Douglas. In 1659 Sherborne Wilson sued Douglas for failing to meet the indenture contract, claiming that Douglas had failed to provide the customary cash payment, clothes, and tools upon Wilson's completion of his apprenticeship. Sherborne, in any case, apprenticed in the New World to an Old World master, but in a trade in which change was not tolerated.

In 1660 Sherborne bought a small lot a few hundred feet down the street from where he had grown up and put a house and a shop on it. The Wilson family had enough means that the young Sherborne could establish himself as a commoner through the purchase of real estate, but it was only because of the importance of his barrels that he was allowed to cut wood from the commons. The town recorded grants to Sherborne Wilson for liberty to fell for his trade more times than to any other artisan; the grants were mostly for white oak, needed for liquid-tight casks. He did receive one for posts and rails, in 1670, and in 1681 the town complained that he had not properly cut up the firewood parts of trees he had felled on the commons.

Wilson sold his house and shop and bought an existing place on the Ipswich River, midway between the two falls. He was living and working there in 1684 when the selectmen requested that Wilson and John Low, "his man," turn out twelve barrels of rotten fish into the river. In 1684 Low was twenty-one years old and either was at the end of his apprenticeship or was a journeyman. The blacksmith John Newmarch testified that he went to Sherborne Wilson's house, "and in the river and upon the shore side he saw a great pa[r]cel of corrupted fish, hake, pollock and haddock."[11] Wilson said they came from the casks that he had rolled down from merchant Samuel Bishop's fence across the river. The rotten fish swirled in the eddies and backwaters just upstream from the mill dam at the Lower Falls. The selectmen clearly thought it simpler to dump almost 2 tons of rotten fish into the river in the heart of the town than to move the barrels to a less offensive place. John Low worked in Ipswich in the 1680s and 1690s. Since Low worked for Wilson the day they dumped the rotten fish in the Ipswich River, it is possible that he could have apprenticed to Wilson, in which case he would have been the second generation trained in the New World. In the 1690s Low had a malt kiln in Chebacco. Every household brewed beer, and malt kilns were monopolies, like the saw-, grain, and fulling mills.

John Kendrick was another busy Ipswich cooper; his career roughly paralleled that of Sherborne Wilson. Like Douglas, he broke town orders several times, a frequent occurrence among artisans. They may have decided that the tree, if big enough, warranted the fine. Like Wilson, Kendrick lived just down the hill from Thomas Dennis on the riverside, a convenient place for an artisan whose trade supplied the shipping interests. When Kendrick saw the Storys loading thatch into their canoes that day in Chebacco in 1668, he himself was loading staves he had made in the woods at the marsh, whence he could conveniently bring them to his house and shop on the Ipswich River. In 1678, Kendrick, his two boys, and George Stimson brought their tools into in the woods near John Burnham Jr.'s and were "working out trees into cooper's ware."[12] They were sawing the trees to the proper length, splitting and riving staves, and, finally, hewing the riven staves with a side hatchet to work them roughly to finished shape. Did the trees grow on common land or private land, and if private, did they belong to John Burnham or John Cogswell? The town found that the trees were public and charged Kendrick thirty shillings. The town took from Kendrick's house a large brass kettle, in which he brewed his beer, to guarantee his paying the fine.

Thomas and Josiah Clarke were father and son. The town knew Thomas as Thomas Clarke at the mill; he lived either in the house that went with the gristmill or near it, which would account for how Josiah quickly returned with the pint of brandy requested by Freegrace Norton. At least three Thomas Clarkes lived in midcentury Ipswich, and later two others joined them. A Thomas Clarke accompanied Winthrop to Ipswich in 1633, and a Thomas Clarke was a carpenter; they were probably one and the same. In any event, the town had enough need for noncommoner Josiah's cooperage that the town allowed Thomas to fell for his son, so long as the cooper sold his wares in town. About the same time, the late 1660s, the town gave two grants to the husbandman Daniel Hovey for his son, James, a cooper, one to make ware and the other to build a shop. In Ipswich at the close of the seventeenth century there were at least five coopers: Sherborne Wilson, John Low, John Kendrick, Josiah Clarke, and James Hovey. Clarke and Hovey benefited from the need the town found for their wares and were encouraged to become residents by offers of wood from the common lands.

Wheelwrights

The wheelwrights, like the coopers, practiced a very specialized trade, and their wheels demanded as much precision and excellence of materials as did casks. The standard wheel of the seventeenth century had been made for several centuries and varied only slightly from wheels made by the Iron Age Celts in Europe five centuries before the Christian era. The wheel had three main wooden parts, the hub, the spokes, and the felloes, five or more of which made up the rim of the wheel. The wheel itself resembled a shallow umbrella: the spokes entered the hubs at a slight angle, thereby increasing the strength of the wheel. The wheels fit on the axle so that the spokes of each wheel were plumb and parallel below the axle and the upper spokes were farther apart. This arrangement gave the wheels resistance to outward pushing force while allowing greater width above the axle for the cart body. Knowledge of the angles of the spokes and the exact shape of the axle descended from generation to generation of wheelwrights.

Each woodworking trade had its own standards of three-dimensional complexity and accuracy. On the one hand, the carpenter was able to visualize and make structures of extraordinary three-dimensional complexity: houses, barns, bridges, and mills had some technical design difficulty to overcome. On the other hand, accurately done carpenters' joinery often showed a gap of $\frac{1}{16}$ inch in finished work. The carpenter needed to work quickly, since time cost money, and did most of his work with tools that might be considered two-handed; the carpenter usually used large tools with as much force as he could. The cooper who made liquid-tight barrels worked to tolerances of several thousands of an inch. But the cooper worked with very small pieces of wood; a stave might weigh only a few pounds, compared with a large timber in a building, which could easily weigh a ton. The wheelwright's work combined the three-dimensional complexity of the carpenter's work with the precision of the cooper. The job of the wheel—to stand up under continual sideways thrusting—depended on the tightness of each joint. Wheelwrights cut their mortise and tenons with such precision that spokes needed to be driven into the hub with a two-handed sledgehammer, the twang of the spoke increasing in pitch with each blow. Although the wheelwright's task demanded accuracy, much of the work used the same two-handed edge tools the carpenter used—axes, adzes, and broad axes—and was highly vigorous.

When the wheelwright finished the wooden part of the wheel, the blacksmith completed the job by covering the outside of the wooden rim with iron. A single, continuous band of iron was known as a tire, but more often the blacksmith shod the wooden rim with short sections of iron called strakes. The wheels saw service on either two-wheeled vehicles, carts, or four-wheeled vehicles, wagons. In England wagons ran on large, long-established farms or in urban areas, places where the roads were well made and maintained; otherwise on inferior farm roads or in mud the cart predominated. In the New World, wheelwrights almost never made wagons in the seventeenth century, since the roads would allow the passage only of carts, which could lumber and wallow through deep, muddy ruts better than wagons. Of the approximately forty grants for wheelwrights' products in the mid-1660s, twenty were for wheels and another ten for a cart or a tumbrel, a cart whose body dumped its load, often manure. In Ipswich, the wheelwright spent most of his time making wheels for ox and horse carts. An iron-shod cart wheel could weigh 200 pounds, and it needed to withstand constant stresses coming from every direction, as when a cart loaded with the usual half ton of firewood lumbered over uneven ground, stumps, and stones. Since a new pair of iron-shod cart wheels could cost two pounds or more, a considerable investment, the wheels needed to last as long as possible; the wheelwright used only the best white oak for the spokes and the felloes, the individual pieces that made up the wooden rim.

In Ipswich, nearly every landowning husbandman owned a cart, and the larger farms no doubt had several. Some individuals, like Freegrace Norton, worth less than the average artisan, owned neither a cart nor draft animals. Some shared ownership, like George Varnum, who died in 1649 owning a team of oxen but only half a cart and half a yoke. Artisans did not all have carts, despite the fact that they all engaged in enough farming to meet their own needs. In Ipswich three pounds would have purchased a good pair of iron-shod wheels and a well-made cart body. Oxen cost about ten to fifteen pounds for a team; indeed, oxen pulled only in a team, from the center of the large, wooden yoke. A single draft horse, however, which cost about three to five pounds, could pull a cart. In addition, oxen and horses needed to be pastured in the summer and fed in the winter. A less well off artisan probably hired plowing and cartage when he needed it instead of owning and maintaining his own vehicle and animals. In any case, there could easily have been several hundred wheeled vehicles in Ipswich toward the end of the seventeenth century, many of which needed repair. The wheelwright also made the stout axles required for such wheels and heavy farm implements like plows and harrows. For instance, the town at different times granted Caleb Kimball trees for wheels, axles, and plows.

Ipswich supported on average four to six wheelwrights during the latter half of the century. The Kimballs, four of whom followed the trade, were the dominant family. Richard Kimball had apprenticed as a wheelwright in Suffolk, England, before he immigrated to Ipswich. His two sons, Richard Jr. and Caleb, to whom Richard Sr. left his tools, also made wheels in Ipswich. Richard Sr. owned a house in the West End, where Richard Jr. probably lived. Caleb purchased a house across the street in 1665, so it is possible that all three worked at their trade at the same time in the same shop for a decade, until Richard Sr.'s death early in 1675 in the Indian wars. In 1690 the town paid Richard £1.05.00 for wheels for the great gun, the town's cannon. John, the fourth Kimball wheelwright, may have been another son, but he lived in another part of town. Finally, about 1700, the town granted John a lot two down from where Caleb lived, the first lot to be cut out of the common fields at that end of town. By that time Richard Sr. had died, but Richard Jr. and Caleb were probably still there.

Turners

Turners worked wood by spinning a piece on a lathe and cutting the rotating wood with a variety of chisels and gouges. The work of turners filled a variety of domestic needs. On one sort of lathe, they turned round, flat objects like plates and bowls and the most common eating dish, the trencher, a plate-sized square of wood with a round hollow turned in it. Pewter, the least expensive of the metals for dining and service utensils, was relatively rare in Ipswich. Everyone but the wealthiest ate off turned wooden dishes and served in turned bowls. Even a modest house had a great number of turned wooden items. Freegrace Norton owned six pieces of table pewter that totaled fourteen shillings and two wooden bowls, three dishes, and six trenchers, all eleven valued at three shillings.

On another sort of lathe, the turner made long, thin objects, like the legs and stretchers of chairs. For hundreds of years turners had made chairs using a traditional method of construction that itself probably went back to the Iron Age. The turner made all the horizontal parts of the chair out of green wood, which he allowed to dry thoroughly and shrink. He turned the four legs of the chair from green wood as well, but while the legs were still green, he bored all the holes in the legs and put the dry horizontals in place. When the legs dried, they then shrank tightly around the already dry tenons. Turners charged considerably less for their chairs than did joiners for theirs, and turned chairs were by far the most common sort of chair in seventeenth-century Ipswich, as they had been in England. Turners also made specialized items, like pulleys for blocks and tackle for ships' rigging, and in a coastal town like Ipswich they spent part of their time servicing maritime needs. Turners also did decorative work, like parts for furniture and balusters for railings. In 1670 the town, responding to the growing scarcity of good white oak, ordered that in the future only wheelwrights, turners, and smiths could get wood for their trades from the commons. Turners, much of whose work consisted of chairs, rarely turned oak for that purpose, using instead white and brown ash, red maple, and poplar, trees of little economic value. The oak granted to the turners was probably for other products that directly serviced the farming and manufacturing interests in the town, like spinning wheels and boat fittings.

Turners in the seventeenth century worked on one of several sorts of lathes, all of them of ancient origins. The turner's leg powered the pole lathe. He stepped down on a treadle from which a strong cord ran up, wrapped a few times around the piece on the lathe being turned, and continued up to the end of a springy sapling overhead. When he trod down upon the treadle, the piece turned toward him, and he cut it with a chisel or gouge. When he took his foot off the treadle, the springy pole returned to its original position, and everything turned in reverse until the turner gave another step down, and the work again turned toward him. Half the time, in other words, the lathe ran backward, and the turner could not turn.

But the pole lathe made up in simplicity and power what it lacked in engineering.

The treadle lathe and the great wheel lathe both provided continuous forward motion. The turner powered the treadle lathe by stepping down on a treadle that was attached to a flywheel and allowed continuous forward motion. The third sort of common lathe was the great wheel lathe. The turner did nothing but turn, while a second person, often an apprentice, cranked the large wheel, which drove the lathe. It is impossible to say what lathe or lathes might have been in an Ipswich shop. The great wheel lathe may have been used only in shops that did very heavy work, like a wheelwright turning large hubs for wheels. Both the pole lathe and the treadle lathe could handle the range of turning commonly done for furniture.

The turner Edward Browne came to Ipswich in the 1630s. He lived in a house in the central part of High Street, another section of small house lots for farmers and artisans, like the West End. When Browne died in 1659, he left in his shop, besides some work on chairs, three finished spinning wheels for linen at 4½ shillings each—indicating that they took about a day and a half to make—and some unfinished wool wheels. Almost every farmer's and artisan's house in Ipswich had a spinning wheel or two to provide the many weavers in town with yarn.

Joseph Browne, Edward's son and also a turner, inherited his father's house and shop, as did Joseph's son, John, who was born in 1674 and worked into the eighteenth century: the same house and shop saw three generations of turners for the better part of a century. From 1663 to 1675 another John Browne, possibly another son of Edward and brother of Joseph, owned a house diagonally across the street from Joseph. Several times in the 1670s the town granted the turners John Browne and Edward Deare trees for their trade. Besides these trees, the town also granted John Browne trees for sleepers for his shop, for posts and rails, to repair a barn and build another, and for fencing, a common handful of uses for an artisan/husbandman.

A few hundred yards east of the Brownes on High Street, twenty-five-year-old turner Edward Deare purchased a house in the mid-1660s, the average age for a young artisan to buy property; in fact, Deare and Thomas

Dennis were about the same age. Deare lived in the house until his death in 1693. John Gaines, a shoemaker, lived next to Deare. Gaines's son, John Jr., became a turner and lived in the house after his father's death. John Jr., who was born in 1677, apprenticed to Deare next door, just as Sherborne Wilson had apprenticed to the next door cooper, William Douglas.

Besides these apprenticed artisans, George Giddings also did turning. A wealthy farmer and a major landowner, Giddings served the town a number of times as a selectman. In 1659 the town allowed Giddings to fell trees for turner's ware and hollow ware, and in 1670 he received a grant for three ash trees, a turner's wood. His turning must have been more than a pastime, for the town treated him as a professional artisan, despite his high social standing.

Joiners

The first artisan in Ipswich to be known specifically as a joiner was William Searle in 1663. Thomas Dennis, who succeeded Searle in 1667, was the second. The town paid each for work. In 1663, the town contracted with newly arrived joiner Searle for four seats "at the two corners of the meetinghouse" worth £5, a substantial sum, equal to a journeyman's yearly salary.[13] In 1681, the town paid Thomas Dennis £1.05.00 for four window frames, probably for the meetinghouse. If these were the only references to the two men, they might be taken for carpenters rather than joiners. For instance, Thomas Waite, a carpenter and once the miller, repaired at town request the meetinghouse seat of Mrs. Cobbit, the minister's wife. His son, Thomas Jr., also a carpenter, built gallery seats in the meetinghouse in 1683 with Nathaniel Lord, another carpenter. The gallery seats were to be made with wainscot, indicating the joiner's frame and panel. The town paid two carpenters, Theophilus Wilson in 1683 and Joseph Fuller in 1690, to make meetinghouse windows.

The activities of carpenters and joiners often overlapped, and certainly carpenters in Ipswich made joined furniture before, and probably after, the arrival of the apprenticed joiners. William Averill, a carpenter, appeared in court in 1659 for failing to fulfill a contract: Averill was to frame an addition, 18 feet on a side, to an existing house and to floor, clapboard, and sheathe it. He was also to make seven windows, both sash and frames, all

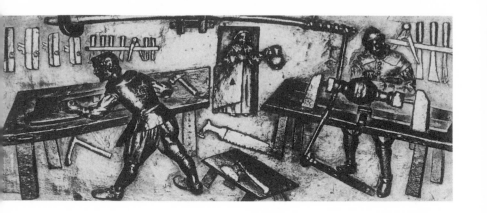

JOINER'S SHOP

A joiner planes a board, held by a toothed gripping device, called the dog, set in the bench top. A second artisan works at a pole lathe, producing what looks like a leg for an elaborate table. Many joiners did their own turning. Between them lies a chopping bench and a hewing hatchet. Either of the two might have used these tools to rough out his work. Tools line the walls: some planes that could be rabbet (edge grooving) or molding (edge decorating); a few chisels, gouges, a pair of dividers; some turning tools and another pair of dividers. The two men could be a master and an apprentice or journeyman. The woman at the door, probably the master's wife, is only a few steps from her house. The jug she carries is filled, no doubt, with beer of her making, since water was generally unfit to drink. By permission of Duncan McNab.

the necessary doors, a 12- to 14-foot-long table and frame, a 4-foot-long joined bench, and a second bench, probably built in, behind the table against the wall. Averill was to do all this work for twelve pounds. He was late, he said, because the owner of the house had not done the work on the foundation he had promised. When Averill died in 1691, he left joiner's tools as well as carpenter's tools. The town paid Abraham Tilton Jr., a carpenter who with his father built the new meetinghouse in 1700, for a communion table for the new building. The six pounds Tilton received for the communion table was half the cost of Averill's whole addition, including doors, windows, and furniture. The younger Tilton may have been a carpenter, but his making of the communion table, a very public piece, indicates that he was probably an accomplished joiner, too.

From 1663 until the early 1690s Searle and then Dennis were the only joiners working in Ipswich. In 1690 Thomas Dennis Jr. was twenty-one years old and beginning his journeyman years. John Dennis was three years behind. In 1693 the town deeded Joseph Whipple, "joiner," 7 acres on the outskirts of the village. Joseph probably had recently finished his apprenticeship, and the grant from the town was encouragement for him to practice in trade in Ipswich. His master is not known.

In 1673 Joseph Browne, a joiner, was born in Chebacco, where he lived his entire life until his death in 1730. Browne finished his apprenticeship in 1694. If Thomas Jr. and John Dennis both apprenticed with their father, which is probable, Thomas Dennis Sr. might not have had the time or resources to accept another apprentice. Browne and Whipple, then, were possibly trained in another town and another shop. Besides Thomas Dennis Sr., suddenly in the 1690s there were three other joiners in Ipswich and one in Chebacco. An increase in work had led to an increase in the number of joiners.

In the beginning years of the town, furniture had been a luxury: resources had first to be put into establishing farmyards and the agricultural landscape. In 1681 in Salem, a major seaport just south of Ipswich, John Tawley, a merchant, commissioned four "wainscot" or joined chests from joiner John Davis of Lynn. Tawley, it turned out, did not pay Davis. One night Davis got drunk and visited Tawley, whom he called "a cheating knave." Davis challenged Tawley to come out of his house and fight. Going inside the house, Davis "took hold of a wainscot chest in the room,

COMENIUS HUSBANDRY

The husbandry engraving from Johann Amos Comenius's *Orbis sensualium pictus* (1658), showing each of the activities that Jonathan Emery was asked to do by his father: plow, 1; plant, 10; harvest, 13; bring to thresh, 16; cut and deliver hay, 22 and 27; and spread manure, 8. For the young Emery, these activities were as complex and experience-rich as his trade.

threw it up and down in the room, breaking several pieces of the front of the chest."[14] Several joiners testified that the chests were worth 25 shillings to 30 shillings each. Since an average plain chest cost about 15 shillings, these joined chests were fairly elaborate, probably as fully decorated as some of the carved chests made by Thomas Dennis.

In 1655 the colony defined "sufficiency" in fencing so that towns would have a standard by which to arbitrate local disputes. The value of a rod— 16½ feet—of sufficient five-rail fence of the sort that would have enclosed the common fields was about 2½ shillings, an average rate in Ipswich for the work. A 25-shilling joined chest, then, was worth the same as 165 feet of good five-rail fence. The amount of fence required to protect only a single acre, about 800 feet, would have cost the equivalent of five elaborate joined chests. Local Ipswich demand for furniture in the early years might have been met by local carpenters and by joiners in other towns, but by the end of the century the town had been established physically, and there was extra to spend on furniture. The population of Ipswich, which had grown steadily throughout the seventeenth century, stood at about 1,200–1,500 in the 1690s, and this greater number of inhabitants itself increased the demand for the joiner's furniture. And finally, the development of foreign markets—Tawley intended to ship the furniture he commissioned from John Davis to Newfoundland—meant that in a seacoast town like Ipswich furniture could have been made for export.

The reality, however, was that Dennis probably did not make elaborate pieces of furniture very often. It was more likely that he worked a good deal on architectural woodwork, like the meetinghouse windows and Searle's seats, and probably turned his hand to many small odd jobs and repairs. In addition to the traditional oak, he may have worked a good deal in white pine and done interior woodwork in that New World softwood. Since Ipswich artisans were at least small farmers, the actual time spent in the shop in a lifetime making the objects that have come to be venerated as icons of the seventeenth century was probably limited in a small agricultural town like Ipswich.

In Newbury, two towns north of Ipswich, the carpenter John Emery made a will. Emery had apparently given half his farm to his eldest son, John, a joiner. The other half he was leaving to another son, Jonathan, a carpenter, so long as Jonathan did certain things for the elder Emery and his wife. Jonathan was to spread manure on his parents' share of the remaining land, both hay meadow and plow land; he was to plow, plant, and harvest the grain for his parents; deliver it to the barn to be threshed; and bring half of the hay he made to his parents. In addition, he had to maintain all the fences protecting the farmland and repair his parents' house and barn. Manuring, plowing, planting, and harvesting were activities any rural artisan knew well. Add to this the maintenance of fences and buildings, not to mention the cutting of firewood, and Jonathan would have been able to work at his trade only part of his time. Searle and Dennis and his sons, no less than their contemporaries, were farmers and artisans.

Chapter Five

Thomas Dennis in the Shop

ON A CLEAR AUTUMN MORNING in early November 1678, Thomas
Dennis, done with some work about his barn and having tended to a few
small repairs to his horse cart, left his house after eating a bite and went to
the shop behind his old house next door. Dennis had lived in the old house
after he married Grace, William Searle's widow, in the fall of 1668, but in
a few years he had built a new house on an adjacent lot. The shop, made
by the cooper Sherborne Wilson about ten years before, had suited Searle
when the joiner immigrated to Ipswich from England and Searle had purchased Wilson's property in 1663. The shop was not large, about 14 feet
by 20 feet, just big enough for a cooper and an apprentice, their tools and
equipment, and a few barrels in the making. Over the years lean-to sheds
had been added to the north and east walls; they now held Dennis's lumber. For the time being the shop was large enough for Dennis, who did
not need much room. Anyway, he would not work in it all day much longer.
Winter was coming, and the shop had no heat, and he would move some
of his work to his new house next door. There he would be warmed by
the large cooking hearth in the hall, a space he would share for the win-

ter with Grace as she went about her daily tasks. Vigorous work, like planing and chopping, he could do in the cold shop, for it warmed his body, but it was much better to carve in front of the hearth fire than to see his breath in his cold shop.

The morning was well under way by now, and the village was beginning to fill with sound. Dennis could hear cow bells here and there and the sounds of chickens and pigs. Up the river to the west a few hundred yards away the gristmill had begun its work, the slapping of the stones muffled but distinct. Down the river from the mill, the cooper Wilson was driving hoops onto a barrel, which echoed like a drum. A little farther beyond, the quick regular blows of a heavy hammer on an anvil came from John Safford's blacksmith shop, followed by a short pause as the smith waited for the iron to reheat in the charcoal fire. At the harborside, due south a short distance, the clear liquid note of caulking irons struck by hard wooden mallets came from the shipyard of Moses Pengry and his sons. Closer to his house, a group of carpenters worked on an addition to a house, hurrying before winter; they, like Dennis, had spent much of their summers at work about their own farms. Dennis could hear the methodical slicing of a log being hewn, the rasping of a crosscut saw, and the thunk of a mortise being chopped. Mingled with the noises of work were the sounds of children playing, a dog barking, and the occasional snatch of conversation. Carts waddled back and forth between the center of town and the river all day long, clanking left then right in the ruts in front of Dennis's house.

Dennis paid the sounds little heed; they were normal and expected in the middle of the week in the busy town. Nor did he remark on the smells—the pitch from the shipyard, the stench of rotten flesh from Hart's tannery on the river if the wind was right, the pleasant smell of Obadiah Wood's bake oven, the wood smoke and animal smells from almost every house. Dennis was thinking about the chest he had to make, a rather fancy one with a carved facade. Now that winter was coming and the farming season was over, he had the time to concentrate on making elaborate pieces. He did make some furniture in the summer, but he preferred smaller jobs, like the repairs he was frequently asked to make on wooden farm equipment that was everywhere in the village in the season they were needed, repairs that could not wait.

  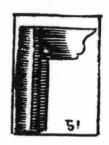

 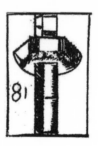 

SOME SEVENTEENTH-CENTURY JOINER'S TOOLS

One of the earliest depictions of common English tools comes from Randall Holmes, *The Academy of Armoury* (London, 1688), a compendium of all the things that appear in a coat of arms, along with brief but illuminating explanations of the purpose of each implement. Thomas Dennis's kit could easily have included the following tools (reading left to right, top to bottom).

Hatchet. "The use of the Hatchet is to hew the Irregularities of such pieces of Stuff, which may be sooner Hewn then either cut with Chissels or Sawn; for that end it is used as an Instrument of Execution for the Beheading of great Offenders, and Rebellious and Irregular Livers: The right side of it. . . . is ground down to a Bevil."

Froe. "An Iron Instrument like a Knife Blade, with a round thick back, having an Eye, into which a thick strong Handle is put, . . . With this, great Timber after it is cloven with the Maul and Wedges into small pieces, it afterwards cleaves them into Laths, Barrell Boards, and Pannels."

Joiner's Square. "It is made of two pieces of Wood, the one Mortessed into the other, and so shot exactly streight as to make a Square."

A Gimlet, a Handsaw, and a Paring Chisel. "The Hand-Bit, of some called a Gimblet, a Piercer, or Nail Piercer, it hath a Worm at the end of the Bit, or half round with sharp edges like the Auger, some for small holes are square in the Bit; of these there are several Sizes." "A Hand-Saw or a Boardsaw; is used by Joyners and other Wood-men, to cut or slit small Timber, as Boards, Spars, Rails, &c." Paring Chisel. "A Chissel with a broad flat, which is not used to be Knockt with a Mallet, but is taken in the hand by the Shank near the top of the Flat, and the top of the Haft or Helve is placed against the right Shoulder, which being pressed hard upon the Haft causeth the edge to cut and pare away."

A Gauge. "Or Oval Gage, or Joyners Gage, is made of either a square, or six square piece of Wood, fitted by a square hole through the middle very stiff upon a Staff, that it may be set nearer or farther off the Tooth at the side end of the said Staff. Its office or use is to strike a Line Parallel to any streight side."

A Jointer Plane and a Foreplane. "A jointer is the largest sort of Plains . . . used, it is perfectly streight from end to end; its office is to follow the Fore-Plane; and to shoot those things perfectly streight." "The Fore-Plain . . . is used to take off the roughness of the Timber before it be worked with the Joynter, or smooth plain. . . The iron or Bit, is not ground upon a streight as other Plains are, but rises with a Convex Arch in the middle of it; and is set also more Ranker."

Smooth Plane. "A short little Plain, which hath its Iron set very fine, and top take off very thin shavings . . . from those Irregularities which the Fore-Plain and the Joynter have left behind them."

Mortise Chisel. "A Chissel broad in the sides and thick in the face part, . . . that it may abide the heavyer Blows with the Mallet, . . .They are of several bignesses answerable to the breadth of the Mortesses they are to make."

Dividers. "A Pair of Screw Dividers, . . . opened and shut with a screw, so that there is noe danger of their moveing, . . . Circles Ovals &c. and also distances are measured and set off from the Rule."

Getting Out the Stock

Dennis looked at his supply of oak, stacked in the shade. He had purchased and felled several large trees earlier that month on private land in the dense woods near Chebacco. Since the town had closed the commons to the cutting of white oak, he, like his master in England, had to buy his trees from private landowners. He tried to visualize in the large bolts the forty or so smaller pieces he would need to make the chest. He had been making furniture for about two decades now and had long since developed the ability to see in his mind's eye how the workpieces would come from his pile of wood. From experience he knew that among the hardest pieces to find would be the panels, the widest pieces in the chest at 10 to 12 inches. Since oak was always split in half and the first split of a log into halves went right through the heart of the tree, a 10-inch panel would need to come from a log more than 2 feet in diameter. One of the trees he had felled was particularly big around. Since the log had split well when he made the bolts, he had decided that he would reserve the bottom few lengths of bolts for panels. These he cut to a bit more than 3 feet in length, in part because a split in a shorter bolt often went more accurately than a split in a longer one and in part because the bottom few feet of a white oak often had particularly difficult grain to separate. He also needed three boards for the top, each about ¾ inch thick, 7 inches wide, and more than 4 feet long. These, too, were hard to find, since they had to be perfect on both sides: the chest top would be seen either closed or open. Dennis could choose from a supply of boards he had made the year before. Top boards needed to be dry to minimize shrinkage between adjacent boards, and if he made them now, they would not be ready in time. But Dennis would make a few anyway, to replace the dry ones he would use. The next most demanding pieces were the stiles, which needed to be about 2 inches thick, 4 inches wide, and almost 3 feet long, and the front and rear rails, which were smaller in section but about 4 feet long. He knew that if he worked up these pieces first, in their making he would find most of the smaller pieces he would need. There was always something left over after he had used a bolt to get out a large workpiece.

For a while Dennis rummaged through his pile of bolts and set aside a few 3-foot-long ones from the bottom of the large tree for the panels and

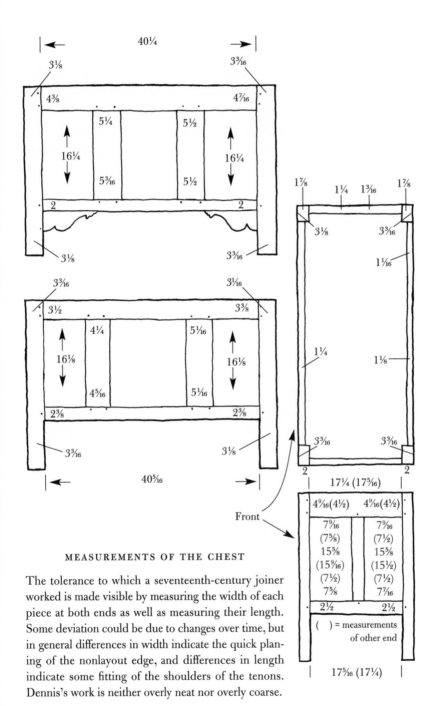

MEASUREMENTS OF THE CHEST

The tolerance to which a seventeenth-century joiner worked is made visible by measuring the width of each piece at both ends as well as measuring their length. Some deviation could be due to changes over time, but in general differences in width indicate the quick planing of the nonlayout edge, and differences in length indicate some fitting of the shoulders of the tenons. Dennis's work is neither overly neat nor overly coarse.

four longer ones from a section of log that was smaller in diameter. From a shop lean-to he got his beetle and wedges and set to work in the yard, splitting the bolts and adding his work sounds to those of the village: the blunt whack of the wooden maul on a wooden wedge, the tearing of the grain if one was nearby, the sharp clout of an ax or hatchet separating the last few reluctant shreds. The more wood he could remove with the wedges, the less work he would have later removing unwanted stock. He examined one of the 3-foot-long panel bolts, deciding whether to split it in half as it was or saw it first into two short pieces. He knew from experience that he could lose valuable wide stock if the split in a long piece should run off at the far end and spoil a possible panel blank. But the wood looked all right to him, so he split the 3-foot panel bolt in half. After a few light blows on the small iron wedge he used to start a split, Dennis heard a distinct crack, and the oak lay open nicely—one face was flat, and the grain separated cleanly. The smell of the white oak, a faint but biting odor of vinegar, went unremarked. He decided, though, that he would use a froe to split the panel stock once more, since with the froe he would have more control of the split; so he set those pieces aside until later.

The bolts for the stiles were not quite thick enough to make two each, but he knew that he would find some rails and muntins in them besides, so he split them with the wedges. Each bolt gave up one piece that would make a stile and a second that would make some lesser parts. But before splitting the bolts into halves, he split off the heart, leaving the bolt with enough width easily to contain the stiles; in these inner pieces, too, he might find some stock, but most often they became fence pales. And just for good measure he split another bolt into quarters, leaving the heart in, for the few small pieces he might not find in the stile and panel bolts. After he had split the stiles out, he turned his attention back to the panel pieces, and with the froe he split the panel bolts carefully and accurately into halves. Despite his best attempts, Dennis was not sure he would get all the wide panels from his rough stock because near the heart of the tree the grain took some awkward twists; when finally planed true and smooth, the panels might not be wide enough. Time would tell.

While Dennis considered the pile of bolts wondering what to split next, his son Thomas Jr. came by to watch. The boy was only nine years old, but he had already shown interest in his father's work; his younger brother,

John, who was six, was still too young to be curious, but he often played happily around the shop while his father worked, and he helped his older brother make playthings. Thomas noticed the older boy looking on and, stopping for a moment, took the opportunity to explain some of what he was doing. Since he was about to split a bolt in half, he told his son how he had to split it right down the middle in order to get two usable pieces. He had done this before; one day it would stick. He showed him why he would choose one end over the other to start the wedge: a small knot near one end would make starting the wedge more difficult and might make the split go erratically. Dennis let his son hold the wedge for him, taking the small hand in his to line the cutting edge up with the rays, which ran from the heart to the bark. He made a few light taps with the maul, being careful not to hit his son's hand. When the wedge caught in the wood, Thomas Jr. pulled his hand away and Dennis gave a more vigorous blow. Then he gave the maul to his son and let him swing. Thomas Jr. could barely lift the maul, and his childish blows did little, but he was earnest. Finally he gave his father the maul and watched as Dennis gave a single blow, opening a crack across the end of the bolt. Dennis put a large, wooden wedge in the crack, set it lightly with a few taps of his maul, and then gave a great blow: the crack sprang down to the knot with a sharp clap; then they both listened as the crack made its own way for a few seconds. Dennis took a second wedge, placed it in the heart edge near the knot, and one more light blow and the piece split in half. Since a few fragments of wood still held the two faces together, Dennis asked his son to get the hatchet from the chopping block. Thomas Jr. carried the sharp tool with some care and watched as his father cut the last wood. They stood for a moment and contemplated their work. Dennis asked his son what kind of oak it was, and his son sniffed and pronounced proudly that it was white oak. Then Thomas Jr. ran off to find his younger brother.

Dennis was pleased at his son's interest; wise, he thought, not to have taken on an apprentice a few years before when the last one had finished. The six- or seven-year commitment to a new apprentice would have meant that his older son would have come of age, about fourteen, before the other's time was up. The thought that his two sons might apprentice with him at the same time pleased him, and there was enough work in the new town to keep them all busy. The small shop, too, needed attention, but it would last until his sons were old enough to help. Like many early buildings in Ipswich, the carpenters framed it as quickly as possible. Instead of making a stone foundation and a full sill into which the posts were tenoned (such a building could last indefinitely if the sills and roof were kept dry), they put the oak posts about 4 feet into the ground to gain stability. In about fifteen or twenty years the rotting posts would need considerable repair. Dennis would have to decide whether to repair his old shop or build a new and probably larger one. But for the time being, he would make do and take no new apprentice. Anyway, the small house was full, and another child living in the place would have made already tight accommodations tighter. Ordinarily his older apprentices would split the stock—a lad of fifteen was getting on to adult strength, and a good and interested one could reason like an adult and not waste much stock. But in the not too far future, Dennis thought, his sons would do it for him. He knew from his own experience in England how important it had been for him as an apprentice to do hard work; it had built his strength and coordination and helped him learn to trust his eye.

Dennis knew the general dimensions of the chest the client had requested—about 1½ feet wide, 2½ feet tall, and 4 feet long. But the precise dimensions would wait until he had his stock in hand; an inch or two one way or another would make no difference, whether a stile was 3½ inches or 4 inches wide, say, or a panel 8 inches or 10 inches wide. From inside the shop Dennis took a coarse-toothed handsaw and his hewing hatchet and went to work on the rough pieces outside in the yard. One at a time he examined each piece. He lifted one end from the ground and sighted along its length, judging for straightness and looking for signs of twist (which could come from a tree whose grain made a gradual spiral up the tree), all the while visualizing whether a bow in the length or twist across the face would allow him to get the dimensions he needed.

Satisfied that the rough pieces were big enough—maybe a few would not do, but he could go back to his pile of bolts later on if he needed—he first cut them roughly to length, about 3 feet for the stiles, 1½ feet for the panels and muntins, and 4 feet for the rails. Then he took the stiles one at a time to the chopping block and worked them with the hatchet to their approximate finished sizes. First he would make one edge straight, usually the edge just under the bark that had the sapwood; the sapwood, he knew, would often be food for various insects and was best removed. When he had made the first edge of each of the stiles straight, he took a small ruler and determined whether he could get a 3¼-inch face from each of them. Finding that he could, he then chopped the opposite edge to the rough width, being careful not to chop too deeply. He examined each stile, determined the better wide face, which would be on the outside of the chest, and hewed that roughly. Finally he removed the inner face to make a piece about 2¼ inches thick. There was a growing pile of chips around the chopping block. Dennis thought that he would have to remind himself to send his boys out to gather them up at the end of the day and pile them in the lean-to, where Grace knew to find what she needed to get her fire going. He did not make as many chips as did the coopers and carpenters in England, who used a much greater amount of wood and were sometimes able to sell their excess, so scarce was fuel wood, but he could keep his wife supplied.

Thomas took the panel pieces into the shop to work on first; he set them on the workbench, which was standing near the wide, south-facing door. Since the wood was green and would shrink in width as it dried, he needed to plane the panel pieces early in the process so that they would be dry in a few weeks, when he would need them. Stacked where they could get a light breeze, they would dry in time, even in November. If he needed them sooner, he could always lean them up in the hearth, where the heat of the fire would dry them soon enough. He also needed to know the width of his panels before he made the rest of the workpieces, because the width of the muntins and the layout of the joinery would depend on the panels' size. He sometimes had extra panel stock lying about the shop, but now the supply was lean.

He also knew that the panels would plane much more easily now, while they were still wet, than if they dried. The more he could do on the chest while the wood was unseasoned, the better. So he set to work first with his foreplane. Because of its size—almost a foot and a half long—and its iron, sharpened to a rounded profile, it made thick, wide shavings. Its length, too, helped flatten the boards, since the cutting iron had to remove the high wood before it could make contact with the rest of the piece. To hold the piece securely, Dennis set the rough panel on the workbench, outside face upward, and drove one end onto the iron dog that protruded from the bench. Along the far edge of the workpiece he placed a thin board between two pins in the bench top, one at the far end. This board kept the panel from moving sideways. Since he needed a perfect face for the outside of the piece, it made sense to make that one first; the inside of the chest could tolerate less perfect stock. Before he began planing, he first looked at the face of the panel piece to see its general shape, holding it up to the blue sky out the door; a slight thickness at one end would have to go first.

Dennis commenced planing. Working diagonally across the oak, he heard for the first few strokes a tick, tick where the plane cut the high spots. Once the small local bumps were gone, he planed with the grain, and the plane would almost shriek as it sheared the green wood; it was a sound he could never get planing dry oak, which would allow only much smaller shavings. When the face of the panel was flattened to his satisfaction, Thomas turned it over on the bench and removed the excess wood from the back, leaving it about ½ inch thick. When he was finished, he had a piece of wood of uniform thickness with one straight edge, the one he had roughly worked on with his hatchet. He checked it with his ruler and decided that it would easily make a panel 10 inches wide, about what he figured he would need. The surfaces of the panel, although reasonably flat, were scalloped from the slightly rounded plane iron. The plane iron also had a nick in its cutting edge, which left a slight bit of unplaned wood the length of each plane stroke. Dennis would give it its final planing later, after it had dried. For this job he would use his smooth plane, a short plane with a lightly set iron that he kept very sharp. The smooth plane would quickly remove the marks of the foreplane and leave a surface ready for finishing. But sometimes he did not get everything, like the inside of the front middle panel of a chest he had made two years earlier, in 1676. He remembered the year because he had carved that date on the front of the chest. He saw the bit of rough planing he had missed when he was giving the chest its final coat of beeswax, and the light caught the oversight just right.

As Dennis worked through the rough panels, the measurements began to become apparent. The end panels, which were relatively narrow, were easily found. But he discovered that some of the wider pieces had troublesome grain at the heart edge, near the inside of the tree: an occasional branch grown early in the tree's life had left a knot, and the grain was too distorted to plane neatly. So instead of making the front panels all the same width, which the stock would not allow, he decided to use the widest panel in the middle. When he had worked up the rough panels he had split out, it became apparent that the big log would not yield enough wide panels; he would be one panel short. Dennis did not want to split another of the large bolts—the wood might dry too much before he needed those pieces.

He could, as he had often done, borrow or swap with someone else; there was always oak in the village. Sometimes, if he had extra, he would bring exceptionally good pieces of white oak to a cooper, who needed the best of stock for his watertight barrels. The ordinaries and inns of the village, where the men would often gather after the evening meal, saw many transactions of this sort. Often there was conversation about politics or about military matters, though there was less of that now that the Indian leader, King Philip, was dead. Dennis had fought in that war. Some men spent too much time in such places, like John Browne, the glazier, who had a habit of drinking more than he should, ignoring his work, and beating his family. So if Dennis needed something, or had something to offer, he knew he could always make a deal of an evening, even if he had to visit several places. But he thought he remembered an exceptionally wide piece of riven oak he had left over from an earlier job. He found it behind his pole lathe, at the entrance to one of the lean-to additions. Dennis could see well enough to turn there. He did not use his lathe as much as a turner, mostly for legs for tables, stools, and chairs; and he gained the space inside his shop. The piece would do, he thought, and he had his panels.

After the midday meal, Dennis returned to his pile of split pieces and pulled out the four stiles. As with the panels, he worked on these first with the hatchet, then with the foreplane. These pieces needed to be reasonably true, since they, like the posts of a house frame, would determine the outside dimensions of the chest. But they did not need to be absolutely perfect. A sixteenth of an inch or even an eighth of an inch difference in width or thickness would be taken up in the final assembly. The eye would likely never see these small variations. Dennis liked to be as neat as the stock would allow, so he tried to plane all the stiles to finished dimensions of 3¼ by 2 inches. The demanding pieces accounted for, Dennis next set to getting out the rails. He needed four long rails for the front and the back and four short ones for the ends. The front rails needed to be good, because these would later be covered with carving; he easily found them.

For the rear rails, however, the stock was not so good. The top rail he finally decided on was near a large knot, and toward the middle of the piece the grain swirled noticeably. But he decided to use it anyway, even though it lacked ¼ inch in width at one end, since he already had so much labor invested in the wood; he could put the worst of the grain on the back of the chest, where it would face the wall.

The afternoon was passing, and with it the daylight. Dennis remembered that Grace had asked him to mend her milking stool, and he still had to tend to a few chores with his animals before dark. So he leaned the stiles and rails against the wall across the shop from the workbench and put away his few tools—the saw hung on a nail over the bench, the planes went on a shelf nearby, and the chisels and other small tools hung in a rack. He took the panel pieces and went to an open shed, where he leaned them against an old barrel in the shade near the entrance; he often put pieces there that he wanted to dry quickly. Dennis went to the small barn nearby to fetch the stool; it would just take a few minutes to make a new leg. He could hear the pig squeal hungrily in the hog cote toward the back of the yard; Grace must have been feeding it the evening meal of scraps and milk left over from her cheese and butter making. Another month and it would be cold enough to butcher. He called for his sons and told them to clean up the shop before it got too dark. They knew where to look near the hearth for the basket in which their mother kept the plane shavings. Although they were green, they were thin enough to dry in a few days; even now the vinegar smell was much reduced. Of all the useful scraps from her husband's shop, to Grace these were the most valuable, a benefit of being a joiner's wife. Of a morning a small handful of dry shavings placed on a few remaining coals in the ashes of the hearth and some gentle blowing would make a bright flame, and the fire would soon be ready for some kindling and wood. She almost never needed more than this to get a fire going because the hearth, her work area, had a fire in it every day of the year, if only for cooking.

Layout and Joinery

The next day Dennis worked on the short framing pieces, the muntins and side rails, also keeping an eye out for pieces for the till inside the chest

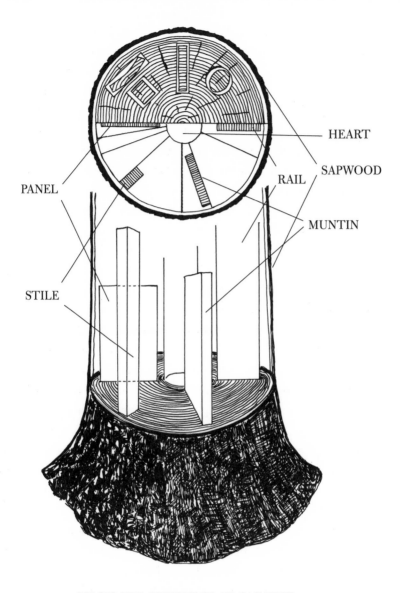

HEART

SAPWOOD

RAIL

PANEL

MUNTIN

STILE

PIECES FOR JOINERY IN AN OAK TREE

The tree trunk (*bottom*) shows how various workpieces—a panel, a stile, a muntin, a rail—fit inside a tree to be riven. They correspond to the pieces in the bottom half of the cross section (*top*). The top half of the cross section shows how pieces from particular places in the log will change shape as they dry. Only the pieces cleft on the radius do not distort as they dry; they only shrink in width and thickness. When Thomas Dennis looked at a tree, this is what he saw. Drawing by Rex Bradeen.

and the bottom boards, which, since they ran from front to back, were short as well. He sorted through the remaining pieces he had split the previous day looking first for rails, which needed to be about 1¼ inches thick, and then for muntins, which could be thinner, since they were mortised into the rails. Dennis's last concern was bottom boards, usually short wide pieces not quite good enough for panels. They needed just one good face, which would be on the inside of the chest; the other face, toward the floor, was of no matter. Only roughly touched by the foreplane, it was still covered with riving marks and chops from a hatchet. Nobody ever looked at the back of the chest, either, which was fortunate. As Dennis worked the stock to the dimensions he had in mind, he realized that he was going to have to make adjustments to his mental image of the back of the chest. His failure the day before to find six panels of adequate width to make up the front and back had altered his plan, but fortunately he had remembered that one wide piece.

Dennis went as far as he could with the muntins and rails in the morning. That afternoon, since he had to change his ideal plans, he would have to go back to all the pieces he had already planed and decide on final measurements. The stiles he knew were fine; he had left the four long rails and the four short rails he had planed the previous day longer than he needed, so they were all right. Since he did not want to shorten the length of the chest, he would have to figure the widths of both the panels and muntins in order to keep the overall dimensions. So Dennis went out to the lean-to and took down the panels he had planed the day before. On the face of the front rails he lightly marked with his scratch awl the locations of the shoulders of the tenons and then took his small square and neatly drew a line; this is where he would saw the shoulders. Dennis set the rails on the bench top and lined up the tenon shoulders on each end with each other, carefully checking that the tenons were in line. He laid the panels on the front rails, the widest in the middle. Accounting for the fact that the panels needed to be ⅝–¾ inch wider than the distance between the muntins—the panels would fit into ½-inch-deep grooves in the muntins— he calculated that he needed two muntins that measured 5½ inches wide. Rechecking the muntins he had planed, he discovered that one would make the needed width but that the other could make only 5¼ inches. Close enough, he thought, and marked the locations for the front muntins on the rails, drew them neatly on the face of the two pieces with the square and scratch awl, and continued those lines onto the edge that would contain the mortise. While he was working with the front rails, he marked the shoulders for the tenons on the ends of the rails all the way around the four sides.

Dennis then marked the tenon locations on the rear rails and set them on the bench top as he had done with the front rails. When he laid the panels on the rails, again with the widest in the middle, he discovered he would need a total muntin width of about 9¼ inches. This worried him because, having gone through the riven stock, he knew that there was little extra. Later in the winter he would have lots of riven bits lying about, but for the time being his supply was low. Only a few weeks earlier he had used all the longer pieces, too thin for workpieces, to rebuild the fence for the hog cote; the heart of white oak made a long-lasting fence pale. So he looked again at his scraps and was just about to open up another bolt when he turned up one piece he had rejected. It had come from a bolt several lengths up the tree, and the heart edge had a large knot. But Dennis judged that he could get the muntin he needed from it; the knot was only on one face, and he could put that toward the back of the chest.

So Dennis planed the muntin and discovered that he could make it about 4¼ inches wide, which would do. He then laid out the back, having all the pieces. But he did not see the square anywhere—he had probably piled something on it—so he marked only with the awl. Since this was the back, freehand lines would be acceptable; he would never do this on a front or end, where the lines would be faintly visible. Dennis then laid out the ends of the chest. They presented no particular difficulty, since the small size of the workpieces allowed a uniformity; all four panels were the same width, as were the pairs of rails and the muntins. Each end would be identical.

By the end of the day he had the locations of the mortises and tenons marked on the workpieces. The next morning, before he could saw the tenons, he needed to saw the rails and muntins to their overall length, about 2½ inches greater than the tenon shoulder to tenon shoulder length. This quickly done, he marked the edges and ends of the workpieces to show where they lay. For this he used a marking gauge, a simple tool with two sharp steel points sticking out slightly from one edge; the distance between

A CLOSEUP OF THE BACK OF THE CHEST

The muntin with the knot is unsightly from this view, but on the inside of the chest it looks good. The upper rail shows a swirl in the grain that was not planed off: to have removed it would have made the piece too thin to be a rail. The panel shows clearly the marks of the hewing hatchet and even the direction of the blows. On the left beveled edge of the panel Dennis left a patch of riven surface. All these tool marks would have been removed on a more visible panel face, including the panels that faced the inside of the chest. The growth rings in the muntin and rail number three or four for each ring in the panel, indicating two different growing environments.

the points was exactly the width of his mortise chisel. With this tool, which he moved along the edge of the workpiece bearing a mortise or tenon, he could scratch two parallel lines at the location of the joinery, within which he would chop the mortises or to which he would saw and split the tenon. In his apprenticeship in England Dennis had learned to use ½-inch-thick tenons set ½ inch back from the front face where the rails met the stiles. For the tenons where the muntins met the rails, he used a ⁵⁄₁₆-inch tenon. Dennis prepared to saw the tenons first. He knew as a practical matter that the oak of the tenons needed to be relatively dry before he pinned the chest together. A tenon became tougher as it dried, and it was better able to withstand the great pressure developed by the pin; mortise and tenon joints pinned while the tenons were still green could become loose as the joint dried. And he knew from experience that the tenons, like the panels, would be dry in a few weeks, about when he would be ready to pin the chest together.

To saw a tenon, Dennis needed the workpiece to be held firmly; if the piece moved, his cuts would be inaccurate, and any gap in the front would be visible on the outside of the chest, where sloppy work could be easily seen. Dennis's method, one of several, was to squeeze the muntin or rail to the bench top with his holdfast. Simplicity itself, the holdfast, shaped like the number seven, was forged from iron. A round shank fit into a slightly larger hole in the bench top. An arm on the top ended in a smoothed foot. Taking the front top rail first, Dennis set it on the bench top, outside face up. He put the shank of the holdfast in a hole and set the foot near the shoulder to be sawn, placing a small scrap of wood on the rail to absorb any deformation the iron foot might cause. Two or three ringing blows from a heavy hammer to the top corner of the holdfast, and the rail was held firmly to the bench top. Dennis took his tenon saw from its nail and began to saw to the line he had scratched on the face. He worked deliberately. Stroke by stroke, he began at the far corner of the shoulder, and as that cut deepened, he gradually brought the saw down until he had sawn all along the scratched line. He tried to split the line in half. The more precise his saw cut here, the less he would have to trim when he fit the joint. He also sawed the front shoulder at a slight angle, making it somewhat less than square. If his cut wandered into the waste wood, it did not matter, because later with his chisel he could trim it to the correct length. But if the saw wandered into the good wood, just on the other side of the line, he would either have a joint that would appear sloppy, or he would have to adjust the other tenons to account for the wood he would lose when he made the tenon square.

When he reached the line, he whacked the back of the holdfast once with the heavy hammer, turned the board over, struck the holdfast two or three times, and went right to sawing the inside shoulder. Some joiners sawed a shoulder and shaped the tenon with a chisel and then turned the board over and did the same; they saved some clamping time. But Dennis liked to do all the sawing at once because he had found that it was important to keep his focus unbroken and intense. Picking up and putting down a chisel and mallet, and the different posture and movements, interrupted for Dennis the fine physical and visual demands of sawing a shoulder clean and square. This inside shoulder he sawed a fraction of an inch inside the line in the wood to be kept. By undercutting the front shoulder, he made it simpler to trim the tenon later in the process; and by undercutting the back shoulder well behind the line, he was ensuring that the back shoulder would never make contact with the stile.

Although he had acquired these habits from his master back in England, where often the wood he had used had dried since being sawn, it was especially useful now that he routinely worked with green wood in New England. As a green stile shrank, he knew, it would change shape: what had once been a perfect rectangle with opposite faces of equal width would become less than perfect, with some corners out of square and the opposing faces no longer the same width. He knew that this change the oak made as it dried was somewhat predictable—he could more or less tell which corner would become greater or lesser than 90 degrees, but prudence was best. And if the inside shoulder should ever touch the drying stile, the force could be great enough to cause the front shoulder to open, resulting in a sloppy-looking joint; it would not be less strong, but it would not be his typical neat work.

After Dennis sawed all thirty shoulders, he readied to make the tenons. Hanging his tenon saw back up, he glanced at the tool rack next to his saws for the chisel he favored for this work, one about ¾ inch wide with a thin blade. Once again using the holdfast, Dennis fixed the first rail he had sawn to the bench top at a place convenient for him to get his body weight behind the chisel, usually at an end. He set the edge of the chisel in the end grain of the tenon a bit above the scribed line and struck it firmly with a mallet. A chip about a third the width of the tenon flew onto the floor. From this first chip, Dennis could judge how the grain wanted to split. In riven wood, which was inherently straight grained, the chip usually would be parallel to the blade of the tenon. But sometimes the split rose into the waste wood, in which case he knew he would have to pare a bit with his chisel to make a flat face. Sometimes the split would work downward, toward the tenon itself, in which case he knew he would have to be careful lest a stray split removed wood from the tenon. But this split went straight, and in a moment Dennis had pared the tenon right down to the scribed line. Since he could easily find the cut line with the edge of his chisel, he knew that the tenon thickness was precise. When he repeated this process on the other side of the rail, he had the first complete tenon. He took the rail from the bench top and checked the front shoulder with the square to see that it lay exactly 90 degrees to the edge; he also, by eye, checked to see that the back tenon was safely out of the way. He went one by one through all his workpieces. In a few hours, he had made thirty tenons; a small pile of chips, which would burn as well as the ones from his chopping block; and some sawdust.

In the afternoon the next task, after sawing the tenons, was to chop the mortises. He did the stiles first, resting them one at a time on the bench top near a bench leg. Since he would drive the mortise chisel with hard blows from a heavy, one-handed mallet, the stiles needed to be held down particularly firmly; again he used his holdfast. The mortise chisel was quite different from the chisel with which he had made his tenons. The blade of that one was relatively thin, only about ⅛ inch thick near the edge and about ¼ inch thick where it met the handle. The mortise chisel was quite thick, almost ½ inch near the edge and ¾ inch at the handle. Since the mortise chisel was thicker at the cutting edge, the sharpened bevel was much longer. He knew that the chisel, as he drove it into the wood between the scribed lines like a nail, would want to follow the bevel into the wood. He started with a few light taps at the middle of the mortise, the flat of the chisel facing him. Then he turned the chisel around, set it about ⅛ inch toward him, and with a few more light taps popped out a small chunk of wood. Then he repeated the operation, this time placing the blade of the chisel about ⅛ inch behind his first blows. Out popped another, larger chunk of wood, making a wider and deeper hole in the waste wood of the mortise. He continued in this fashion, chopping from each end, until he had reached 1½ inches in depth and only the ends of the mortise remained to be chopped. He worked on each end one at a time, gradually chopping toward the end of the mortise. He could judge by eye whether the mortise was parallel with the face of the stile. He simply lined up the mortise chisel with the front edge of the mortise. The chips, which with the first few pairs of blows had popped out easily, now became stuck in the mortise; to get them out, he had to lever on the end of the mortise and pry the chips out. Finally, when he had come to the end of the mortise, he took one final blow, the flat side of the chisel toward him. He held the chisel at an angle so that the last chop undercut the end, making the bottom of the mortise longer than the opening on the face of the stile. Since he had gone a bit past square, the tenon could not get caught in the mortise, held out by excess wood at the ends of the mortise. To pry loose the last chip, Dennis pulled back strongly on the chisel, levering on the top of the mortise. The wood at the top buckled slightly, but Dennis just left it, as was common practice. The slight bulge did not interfere with the joinery, and the client did not notice.

The mortises took somewhat longer to make than had the tenons, and he worked much harder. After the first mortise he removed his doublet, which he hung on a nail by the door. Chopping mortises, unlike sawing tenons, was strenuous work. But he had learned in his youth that at the right pace he could work for many hours. Too fast, and he would tire quickly; too slow, and the job was delayed. Too big a bite, and the chips clogged the mortise, taking longer to clean out than if he had chopped more methodically. Dennis liked to do all the mortising at a single session, so he worked steadily and was done by evening.

The fourth day, the tenons and mortises done, Dennis set about the rest of the work. Before he could fit the joints for the final pinning together, the last task before the carving, he had a bit more joinery to do: plane grooves for the panels and grooves for the bottom boards. He took his plow plane from the shelf holding his planes, checked that the iron was the needed 3/16 inch, and set the fence to plane the groove ½ inch from the front face. The plow plane is simple in use: a workpiece, like a muntin, is held edge up, and the joiner pushes the plane forward from the near end.

Dennis used a simple device to hold his workpieces upright. On the left end of the front of his bench a horizontal hook was bolted to the bench top. The front legs each had rows of holes from top to bottom. By placing pins in these holes at the proper height, Dennis could firmly support the bottom of the board. When he pushed the plow plane forward, the force pushed it tightly into the vee where the hook and bench top met, and the piece was secure. Like the holdfast and the bench dog, this device required no moving parts and was quick to use and simple to maintain.

After a few strokes, he was making shavings the length of the muntin, thick enough to tie into a knot. After about two dozen quick strokes, the groove was the required ½ inch deep. Dennis worked through the framing pieces, finishing with the stiles, which presented a particular problem. When he worked the plow plane from end to end of the muntins and rails, the groove ran right through the tenons. But were he to do the same on the stiles, he would have left a part of the groove on the top of the stile, at once weakening the integrity of the oak so near a mortise and making the top of the stile unsightly (see the illustration of the draw bore in the Introduction). Since the plow plane only worked forward, it was inherently right-handed: Dennis could plane only from left to right. If he started with the bottom mortise, he could end his stroke with the front of the plow plane resting in the previously chopped mortise for the wide top rail, but he had to plane below the narrow bottom mortise to get the groove deep enough. If he started from the top mortise, the bottom of the plane kept the iron from engaging the wood completely, and in order not to harm the wood on the top of the stile, the groove did not reach its full depth until about a foot down. So he had to clean out the groove with a ³⁄₁₆-inch mortise chisel to its full ½-inch depth. Most joiners did this, leaving a partially plowed groove below the bottom rail that only an observant owner would see and would understand why it was there.

That afternoon, the panel grooves plowed, Dennis replaced the ³⁄₁₆-inch iron with a ½-inch one and set the fence at ¼ inch. He plowed a groove on the inside of the bottom of the front rail: into this groove would fit the ½-inch-thick bottom boards. The bottom of the lower side rails were ¼ inch

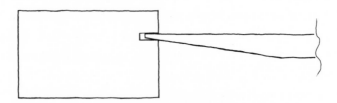

PANEL AND GROOVE

The panel does not contact the bottom of the groove. As the panel expands in the damp summer and shrinks in the dry winter, the space affords room for movement. As with pins, panels were never glued. If they were fixed in their width, they could either buckle in damp seasons or, restrained from shrinking, crack in dry seasons.

BRACKET

Many Dennis shop chests had brackets with this same sequence of shapes, but no two are the same length. So familiar was Dennis with this shape that he probably just drew it quickly on a piece that happened to be about long enough.

higher than the bottom of the front rail, and on the insides of the lower side rails he planed a rabbet (a groove at the edge of a board), this time using a plane designed specifically for that task. The bottom of the lower rear rails was ½ inch higher than the bottom of the lower front rail. Thus, the bottom boards could be installed easily in the assembled chest: the fronts fit into the groove; the end boards sat in the ½-inch rabbet; and the back ends of the boards he merely nailed onto the bottom of the rear rails. He had taken pains to plane neatly only the tops of the bottom boards, leaving the undersides—invisible unless the chest was turned over—rough and uneven. Since he used short nails for this job, he scooped out with a carving gouge a bit of wood for the nail to fit in.

The grooves done, Dennis turned his attention to the trial fitting of the frame. In order to be able to lay out the holes for the draw bore in the tenons, he first bored the holes in the mortises, using a ⅜-inch bit for the stiles and a ¼-inch one for the rails. The type of bit he used, called a gimlet, began with a small screw at the point and then increased in diameter for about an inch until it reached its intended diameter; this bit bored a tapered hole, full size on the outside surface and smaller where it exited the wood. Then he took all the pieces that made up the front—the two stiles, two rails, and two muntins—and checked how each joint fit together. Some tenons were a bit thick, and he had to pare some wood off the tenons with a sharp ¾-inch chisel. The mortises were wide enough—the width of the mortise chisel established that—but sometimes the chisel followed the grain, and the mortises were not square to the surface, so he pared, again with his ¾-inch chisel, to allow the tenons to sit squarely with the mortise. He had sawed the shoulders carefully, and they all looked good to his eye, but he knew that when he preassembled an entire side he could expect a few of the joints to be open slightly. Sometimes the wood had changed shape a bit; sometimes, in either planing the mortise edge or sawing the tenon, he was off a bit. A very small discrepancy did not bother him: he knew that the force of the draw bore pin would close up small gaps. But a few he worked on a little, usually taking some off the shoulder of the tenon. The result was that two framing pieces that should be identical in length—the two rails, say, on the same face—varied by a small amount, less than ¹⁄₁₆ inch. No one would ever see this (unless carefully measuring with a ruler), and the joints would all appear tight and strong. Joiners everywhere worked this way, of course, since their profit came from their speed. Satisfied with the fit of the front face, Dennis marked the centers of the pin holes on the tenons and took the front apart. He proceeded in similar fashion until he had fit all four sides. To bore the holes in the tenons he knelt on the work-piece on a low bench and set the point of the gimlet bit about ⅟₁₆ inch closer to the shoulder, a distance his master had described as the thickness of a shilling. But night was coming, so he cleaned up his shop and went into the house for dinner.

The fifth day Dennis had a few details that needed attention before he could put the chest together, and he typically did all the work before he started the carving. Under each end of the front bottom rail he commonly used a bracket. On this chest, each tapered from about 4 inches next to the stile to almost nothing about 10 inches out. The brackets moved toward the center of the chest in a series of curves. The end of the bracket fit into a mortise in the stile, but Dennis never put a pin in this joint, as it would add nothing to the strength of the frame. Rather, he relied on a single nail, driven through the bracket near the thin end into the underside of the bottom rail. He had made the tenons on the ends of the brackets while he was sawing the others, one on each end of a suitably wide and long board. Now he sawed the curves so the brackets would be ready for carving. Dennis was not fussy about the bracket dimensions, and although the brackets on a given chest were of identical dimensions, they varied from chest to chest. He knew the sequence of curves so well that he could lay out a bracket quickly. Indeed, Ipswich residents would recognize the unique design as his, since his brackets were always the same sequence of curves. He cut the curves on one bracket quickly with his bow saw—a narrow blade tensioned in a wood frame—then traced the curves on the other bracket, and sawed that.

He needed two cleats for the ends of the top, almost as long as the top was wide, which he fitted onto the underside of the top. Since he planned to use three riven oak boards for the top of this chest, the purpose of the cleat was to keep the ends of the boards registered with each other as well as to keep them together. Dennis would not glue the oak boards together to make a single, unbroken top; joiners simply used the occasional dowel or loose rectangular tenon in the edges of adjacent boards to line the surfaces up, and they let the cracks between the boards expand and contract as they pleased. For oak tops like this Dennis typically fastened the boards to the cleats with oak pins. Had this chest had a single-board pine top, the main function of the cleats would have been to keep the top flat. The two cleats were not large, about an inch square. These he made as he always had: the front ended in a shallow ogee (an S or reverse) curve about 2½ inches long, demarcated from the rest of the cleat by a shallow vee. Like the brackets, the design of the ends of the cleats was distinctively his.

This chest would have a till, a small box built into the inside, on the upper right-hand side as one opened the chest and looked in. He needed three thin boards: a bottom, a front, and a top; the ends and back were simply the inside of the chest. The bottom and front were set in grooves in the framing pieces, and the top hinged on two pins, worked on each end and fit into holes bored in the stiles. Dennis set the till top at a slight angle, a custom of his, and yet another characteristic of his work; most other joiners made flat till tops.

The only task left was to work some moldings on the framing pieces. Dennis had a variety of molding planes, including about half a dozen different ogee widths, from ½ inch wide, which he often used on furniture, to a large one of about 2 inches, which he used for architectural work. Like all joiners and carpenters, Dennis bought the irons and made the wooden body, about a half day's job. He also made much use of a scratch stock, a hand-sized L-shaped piece of wood. One leg rides along the edge of the piece to be molded, and the other extends over the face. This leg had a saw run through it vertically, into which slit was tightly fastened a piece of steel (often an old saw blade), on the bottom of which was the profile to be scratched. By pushing down and forward on the scratch stock the joiner gradually deepened the cut until the full design appeared.

On this chest Dennis scratched a channel mold, a flat recess bounded on each edge by a small quarter-round element, on the top and bottom rails on each end, about in the middle of the width. Between the channel mold and the edge of the rail next to the panel, he scratched a design particular to his shop, one he had picked up in Ottery St. Mary: a small ogee preceded by two vees. A convenience of the scratch stock was that, by loosening a few screws and sliding the iron along the stock arm, it could easily place the molding any distance from the edge, but the cut it made was not as clean or consistent as that of a plane, and it took longer.

But the other molding on the chest occurred on the edge of the wood, and for these Dennis used his molding planes, designed to run on the edge. On the edges of both the front and end muntins he started to work with an ogee plane about ⅝ inch wide but stopped planning when he had cut a shallow, round groove about ½ inch in from the edge. From this groove he planed a flat bevel down almost to the panel groove; the effect was to frame the panel, as though it were a picture. He worked the same molding on the front edge of the till top and used the small ogee plane to work the upper edge of the bottom till board, a bit of decoration for the inside, and it only took a moment.

By the end of the day, all the workpieces prepared, Dennis was ready to carve. It had taken him about forty hours, a modern workweek, to do the joinery. The carving would take about as long, almost doubling the cost of the chest to the client. The carving was the last thing Dennis would do before he assembled the piece. The work was much more easily done on one piece at a time on his bench top than it would have been to carve the whole assembled front: he often needed to have the weight of his body right over a tool to carve accurately.

Carving

While Dennis was doing the joinery on the chest, he was considering the carving, not so much in words, but rather, from time to time, images would come into his mind. The stiles, rails, and muntins were not much of a question: for these parts he had the choice of a number of standard designs, easily altered in either width or length. The panels he found himself wondering about. Growing up in Devon, he had seen much carving, some of it found everywhere in England, some only locally. In Ottery St. Mary, where he apprenticed, he learned how to design as his master had designed. In St. Mary's Church, where he went with his master and his family, the ends of the pews had been carved more than a century before with a design that would influence much local carving: a long, narrow panel contained a round vase out of which climbed a vertical spray of flowers and foliage. This design had been used by generations of local carvers before Dennis, each of whom found his own version. Young Dennis absorbed the sense of the church pews and saw not only the carving of his master but also, in almost every house he went into, locally carved furniture.

When Dennis carved panels, he approached each piece of furniture anew, and no two came out exactly the same. Sometimes he would alter the main design elements using different ones here or there or using different details on similar elements. Small spaces of an inch or two he might fill with any of a number of details. The time spent in his youth looking and carving had allowed him to develop his own style within Devon carving, one he was so familiar with that he could improvise as he carved. Since William Searle and Thomas Dennis were the first professional joiners in Ipswich, there probably was not much carved furniture in the town. Many of Dennis's townsmen were from the east of England and had grown up used to carving different from Dennis's west of England style, but they seemed to appreciate his work enough that he was often asked to carve a

THE OTTERY ST. MARY'S PEW END

The end of each pew lining the aisle of the church has an identical carving, dating from 1526. The motif of interwoven flowers on long stems springing from the mouth of a round, handled jug is common in Devon work, as are stylized variants, and this church pew, seen by many generations of joiners, could easily have been responsible. Tracing from photograph by Rob Tarule.

TWO DENNIS GREAT CHAIR BACKS

The great chair, descended from the throne and the possession of the master of the house, was often carved. The chair back on the left (which is part of the Bowdoun College Museum collection) has a clearly depicted jug and springing stems. The two round flowers are quite similar to other carvings in St. Mary's Church. (Some background carving has been left out to show more clearly the main design elements.) On the chair back on the right (part of the Peabody Essex Museum collection) the stems spring from a stylized circular jug mouth. Variants of both—the complete jug and the stylized jug mouth—appear in Dennis's other work. Tracing from photograph by Rob Tarule.

Devon-style piece. The night before he began to carve, falling asleep, he saw the finished design.

In the morning Dennis began by laying out all the carving. As with the layout of the joinery, he did all his planning at a single time, so that when he went to work, he could do so without stopping to think. First, he put boundary lines on all the workpieces to contain the carving. One-half inch in from the end of each framing piece he scratched a line with an awl and square (just as he had done to lay out the joinery); with a marking gauge he struck other lines ½ inch in from the parallel, long edges. On the panels he cut similar lines, so that the carving was bounded by a ½-inch frame.

The rails and muntins he laid out with a pair of dividers. The dividers allowed him to locate the design elements without using a ruler to measure and without doing any arithmetic. For the top rail he had decided on overlapping half circles, called lunettes. He set the dividers to the distance between the top and bottom boundary lines, about 3½ inches, put one leg on the vertical midline, the other point on the boundary line, and, using that point as the center, scratched a semicircle. He continued in both directions from the midline until he had covered the whole length. Then he drew a second set of semicircles that equally overlapped the first set. Setting the dividers to ½ inch less, he drew a second set of semicircles inside the first set. Finally, with the awl and square, he cut vertical lines that sprang from the centers of the semicircles. The bottom rail he divided into eight equal sections: he set the dividers to what he guessed was correct and stepped off from the midline four times. When he got to the end, he saw he was a fraction of an inch short of the end boundary line, so he widened the dividers a bit and stepped off again, still found it not quite right, adjusted once more, and this time came out close enough. He then cut vertical lines that divided the rail into eight equal sections. The design of the rails was horizontal; for the muntins, vertical. First, he cut a vertical centerline and then with the dividers apportioned the vertical distance into quarters. On the bottom rail and muntins the lines established the ends of the series of S curves.

For the stiles Dennis used another motif. The major element was two vertical stylized leaves, the top one about half as long at the bottom. For these, besides the boundary lines, he first marked a vertical centerline to locate the central veins of the leaves. Then he set the dividers to the distance

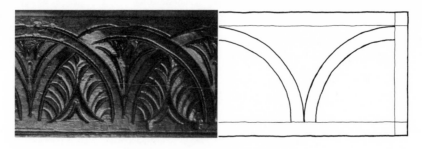

THE TOP RAIL OF THE CHEST

Straight lines and scribed compass arcs provide the needed references
for the carving.

between the side boundary lines, and at the top of each stile he drew a semicircle so that it was in line with the smaller circles on the lunettes of the top
rail. About one-third down the stile he drew a circle and inside this a second circle with a radius about ½ inch smaller. This circle determined the
bottom of the top leaf and the top of the bottom leaf.

The panels he approached differently. The wider central panel was a bit
different from the two end panels, but they shared many major elements.
Each was divided vertically into halves. With his dividers he drew a circle
at the top, the diameter equal to the distance between the boundary lines,
and tangent to both the top and the sides. Inside this he drew a second
circle, ½ inch smaller in radius. Since the center panel was wider than the
identical end panels, he needed two different settings and did the end panels together.

Dennis left his workbench by the door and went to the back of the
shop to get his rolls of carving tools from the storage shelves on the win-
dowless north wall. It was dark back there, behind stacks of boards and
other odds and ends, but he knew where everything was. Back at the workbench he opened a roll and looked at the gouges, each a different width
and bearing a slightly different curve. Were he to push an edge straight
down into a piece of wood, move it a bit less than the width of the blade,
line up the curves, and push it down again, and continue this a few more
times, he would make a circle distinct to that particular gouge. Most of
his gouges would make circles between ¼ inch and 2 inches; a few were
bigger. He was looking for one particular gouge that made a circle ⅝ inch

THE MUNTIN OF THE CHEST

Straight lines and a growing pattern of arcs of circles generated by different gouges driven straight down define the primary pattern. The layout of the muntin shows the sequence the carver might have followed. First the ends and the small circles were defined by the gouges, then the reverse curves were done with the V tool (possible by eye, with no further layout), and finally the leaves inside the ends were chopped by the gouge.

THE CENTER PANEL OF THE CHEST

Scribed arcs and straight lines define most of the design. The leaves and flowers, both major and minor, are forms that show up again and again in Dennis's carving. Note the stylized jug mouth at the bottom. A frequent carver like Dennis could elaborately fill the framework of the design with any number of details.

in diameter. The gouge had come with him from England, one of the tools his master had given him when he finished his apprenticeship. Others he had purchased in England before he emigrated, knowing they would cost less there. A few special carving tools he had bought in Ipswich from local merchants—usually well stocked with tools from England—who had ordered them for him from England; he might wait many months for a tool to arrive. Ipswich blacksmiths, like their other New World peers, were too busy making the necessary iron work for agriculture and commerce to gain the skill, expertise, and equipment of a specialist toolmaker in England. Some New England blacksmiths made fairly coarse tools, like many used by coopers and carpenters. Fine tools, like chisels, plane blades, carving gouges, and handsaws, came primarily from England. Those New England blacksmiths trained in fine work did gunsmithing, so important were weapons in the new settlements.

Opening a second roll, Dennis found the gouge he was looking for. He began with the muntins. He set the ⅝-inch gouge about ½ inch from the corner formed by the end and boundary lines and made eight small circles, striking straight down on the vertical tool with his wooden carving mallet. Next he took a gouge that made a 2-inch circle and, at the ends of each pair of crossed curves, made downward blows between the ends of the S curves and between their middles and the boundary lines.

Dennis next took his V tool, the cutting edge of which was shaped like the letter *V,* and by eye, neatly driving the V tool with light mallet blows, cut the edges of the S curves, leaving about ¼ inch of surface between them. Dennis found in his tool roll the gouge he always used to remove the background of his carving, one based on a 2-inch circle and only about 5⁄16 inch wide. With this gouge he removed the background to a depth of about ⅛ inch, the depth to which the V tool and gouges had cut. When he was done, the ⅝-inch circles and the space between the leaves became obvious. Then he took his V tool again and added some secondary curves and finally took up the 2-inch gouge again and added a few details with a single, downward blow. When he finished both muntins, he took a small punch whose end was about ⅛ inch round (he had quickly made it years ago by filing a nail to the shape he needed) and punched a number of final decorative details on the carving.

When Dennis trained in Ottery St. Mary, he learned a formal, intricate sort of carving, called strapwork, in which regular geometric shapes of 2–4 inches, mostly circular, square, or rectangular, repeated in succession across the carving. For this work he needed specialized gouges that came in precisely matched series. To make a circle around a ⅝-inch circle and leave ⅜ inch of surface, a gouge that made a 1⅜-inch circle was needed. With enough gouges, a carver could neatly fill spaces of any dimension. Among Dennis's carving tools were many gouges devoted to this sort of complex carving. He was not doing any of that carving on this chest, although he often found call for it in Ipswich. But the small circles and leaves he quickly made on the muntins derived from this sort of carving. The V tool allowed Dennis another sort of curved line, either too big for a gouge or based on an ellipse and not a circle. The V tool allowed him to make the S curves.

It took Dennis about a day and a half to carve the framing pieces; the panels would take about as long. The days were short now that it was November, and he often carved in the house, where he used the end of the eating table as a workbench. Even then, in front of the fire and near a south-facing window, he could not work much more than eight hours a day, less if it was cloudy.

Dennis carved the center panel first, starting with the V tool. His goal at this point was to separate major elements from the background. First he carved the large semicircles at the top. These were the most difficult to make look good, since both paired circles had to be consistent, parallel, and fair curves. He could go off a bit on a leaf or flower and the eye would not see the differences, but if his V tool went off on a large circle, the variance would stand out. The semicircles presented another problem: different grain. Since the riven panel went almost from the heart of the tree to the bark, all different rates of growth occurred on the same piece. Where growth was slow and the rings close together, carving was easier in the relatively porous wood. Where growth was more rapid and the rings wider, the wood was harder. Dennis proceeded by making lots of light blows, often going no more than ¹⁄₁₆ inch each time. This way, were he to stray, he would not go far. Dennis had constantly to alter the force of his blows and the angle of the chisel, lest he go too deep or too shallow or wander from the scribed line as the V tool suddenly took off into soft wood.

BOX FRONT CARVED IN THE MANNERIST MODE

All boundaries between the foreground and background are defined only with gouges and straight-edged chisels. Making the two edges of the large circle in the middle required two matched tools. The only V tool work is the spirals in the corners.

The semicircle done, he moved to the other shapes—leaves, flowers, stems, the vase at the bottom. Finally, he carved the boundary lines.

Dennis then chopped straight down on his 2-inch and 1½-inch gouges, outlining the flowers, leaf ends, and other small details. When he was finished, he had demarcated the foreground from the background. Next he removed all the background, and the design appeared in two dimensions. Most of the work was now done, and he had only to add smaller details, sometimes making additional highlights with the V tool, sometimes with various gouges. He worked with one tool at a time, so that he picked up and put down his tools the least. Then he rounded some of the surfaces—leaves, flowers, stems, and the large circle—carefully paring the wood from the surface to the background. These curved surfaces would catch and reflect light. The final step, after the carving was done, was to punch the small ⅛-inch circles and some dots, for which he used a punch that came to a point. He stamped the large circle on the top every inch or so and here and there on leaves and flowers, one last additional texture.

The center panel done, Dennis went on to the two end panels and proceeded in the same manner as he had for the center panel. Again, he finished by punching the small circles and dots. These he did by eye, without laying out. In each of the large circles at the tops of the end panels he punched nineteen small circles, and he added two dots at the ends of the leaves inside the large circle. On the center panel, however, he had put twenty-three dots on the large circle and no small dots on the leaves. Also on the center panel he had punched a dot in the center of the small leaves in the upper corners but not in the same element on the end panels. Were these small differences intentional and planned, a small variation to pique the interest of the viewer? Or were they the result of working quickly in poor light at the end of a long day? Or were they just how a traditional artisan worked, each recasting just a bit different?

The last bit of design Dennis did before assembling the chest was to pick out some of the background with pigments mixed with linseed oil and a small amount of turpentine. He painted the background of the muntins and bottom rail black, and on the panels he painted the background at the top and bottom vermillion and the middle part black. The black he made by grinding charcoal; the vermillion was imported from England. The color enhanced the sense of the carving by making it stand out even more, the better to be seen in a dim seventeenth-century Ipswich room.

When the linseed oil paint was dry, in about a week (black was slow to dry), Dennis finally assembled the chest. He had already done his last fitting and the draw boring. He had been making pins—he needed about seventy—right along in odd moments too small to fill with a larger job. Fine-grained oak, like most of the wood Dennis used, did not make good pins. It was a bit brittle, and when he chopped the pins off flush with the surface after they were driven in, often a clump of grain pulled out of the middle, leaving a blemish. So he saved scraps of coarser-grained oak as he came upon them. About eight or ten rings per inch yielded about the toughest oak. Dennis split pieces several feet long into rough pin blanks not much bigger than the pins; these he could whittle with a sharp knife or chisel to the proper taper. The assembly went quickly, and he was done in a few hours. He put the chest together in the house because he still needed to give it a few thin coats of linseed oil followed by a few coats of beeswax dissolved in turpentine, and the warmth in the room aided the drying. The owner came to Dennis's house to approve the chest. He had not doubted Dennis's craftsmanship—he knew his work well—and was as pleased as Dennis with the result. They agreed that two Saturdays hence he would come again, settle up, and help Dennis load the chest on his horse cart for the delivery across town.

Epilogue

WHEN THOMAS DENNIS DIED in 1706, he held the office of tithing-man, a fitting conclusion to his life as an artisan in late-seventeenth-century New England. Both roles were public. At his death, he was one of the town's "most prudent and discreet Inhabitants."[1] As a younger man he had been sued by his stepchildren, brought to court by the town, and fined for angrily impugning the honesty of a local merchant. He spent eight days per year training with the Ipswich militia and fought in King Philip's War, a short, difficult, and brutal winter war, one of about 120 Ipswich men, more than a dozen of whom were killed. He enforced the town's laws as a constable and collected a sudden thirtyfold increase in colony taxes. He was a good father, according to his neighbors. He was of average wealth.

Perhaps most noteworthy from our standpoint, he was the last of his sort. The techniques he knew—how to work with unseasoned oak and how to split the oak from logs—were no longer needed, as the making of furniture shifted quickly to the skills of the cabinetmaker, who used wide, carefully dried sawn boards. The cabinetmaker's work may have been quicker, but there was more to the public acceptance of the new trade than expense. Cabinet work provided a new look: large areas of flat wood replaced the two dimensions of the joiner's work, and light-colored woods, many with pronounced grain thought to be attractive, replaced the rectilinear furniture the joiner made. The interior of rooms became lighter as window glass decreased in expense, and new architectural styles used many more windows than had those of the early seventeenth century. Ceilings became higher, began to be painted white, and plastered and painted walls replaced much of the earlier wood paneling. The new, light-colored and vertically oriented furniture of the cabinetmaker was thought to be more appropriate to the new architecture.

Furthermore, carving was already becoming obsolete when Dennis apprenticed, and a new decoration for joined furniture, which used many complex moldings and turnings, was becoming popular. Both these styles, carved and mannerist, belonged to joined furniture and were well suited to the dimly lit interiors of seventeenth-century houses, in which the extravagance of a finely figured wood could not easily be seen and appreciated. The carving and molding of the joiner were less subtle and showed up well in dim, flickering light. Dennis's sons could have learned both skills, the mortise and tenon of the joiner and the dovetails of the cabinetmaker, but Dennis's grandson, John, probably worked mostly with wide, dry boards. The mortise and tenon joint continued in use—carpenters framed houses using this technique until the end of the third quarter of the nineteenth century—but the joint assumed a supporting, if useful, role in furniture construction. Oak, too, fell from favor as a furniture wood, and it was not until the end of the nineteenth century that it appeared again, in the work of the Arts and Crafts movement, which saw in oak a metaphor for the presumed virtues of the seventeenth century—hard work, strength, and forthrightness. Dennis's woodworking descendants needed to supply clients with the furniture they wanted, and no one wanted joined furniture any more.

Ipswich, too, changed. The landscape, increasingly converted to agricultural land, grew fewer and fewer trees. The cutting of the forests and the increasing agriculture allowed more soil to wash into the Ipswich River, until the harbor silted in and even the small, coast-wise ships could no longer sail into town. Ipswich gradually became something of a backwater town as trade moved to larger, deepwater ports. Ironically, a similar fate befell Plymouth, the Pilgrims' choice. Plymouth Harbor had never been deep, and the town supported only a fishing fleet. By the middle of the twentieth century, Ipswich and Plymouth had the largest stock of extant seventeenth-century and early-eighteenth-century houses in New England, not because of any love for the past but because the local economies provided little surplus wealth, and the inhabitants were forced to repair the old instead of building new, grander houses. Plymouth, unfortunately, was struck by urban renewal in the 1960s, and the largest single neighborhood of seventeenth-century and early-eighteenth-century houses in New England was demolished. Ipswich was still too poor to support urban renewal, and its old houses escaped, leaving the town now with the largest collection of early buildings in the New World.

Beginning in the early eighteenth century, those who could afford new furniture bought cabinet work. Gradually, the old-fashioned joined furniture left the main rooms. Some made it to back rooms, the upper floor, or the attic, to continue useful and easy lives as storage. Some furniture moved to the work rooms or even the barn. A farm wife, on her way to the dooryard to feed the chickens, might stop in the dimly lighted lean-to addition beyond the kitchen. She lifted the lid of the old chest, balancing it carefully against the wall. One hinge was broken and probably had been since her grandmother owned the piece. The farm wife reached in and felt in the darkness for the bag of old Indian corn for the chickens. It was too dark to see the carving that covered the chest's front, once noticed by all who came into the hall, the main room, of her great-great-grandmother's old house. The wife noticed that the mice were back; time to have her husband nail another patch over the hole when he returned from plowing. Kindling, she thought absent-mindedly, looking at the chest, and shut the worn lid.

But the Dennis chest spent a peaceful century and a half in its house, perhaps in the attic, where it might have kept old but still useful clothes or family heirlooms. It was not opened very often during that time; occasionally someone put things in or took things out. The unheated room the chest might have occupied was small. It was right under the roof, and there was only one little window. The household used the room for storage, and things were constantly rearranged by season. In the fall there might be barrels of grain and wool waiting to be spun during the winter, and in the spring the looms, on which the family wove in a warm room downstairs in the winter, might be disassembled and piled with the chest. For generations family members put things on the chest while they rummaged about, and they leaned things against it. The chest's bright paint was getting shabby.

The chest never left Ipswich. Until the middle of the nineteenth century it saw some service, but not nearly enough to wear it out. Then one day the family members emptied the chest and brought it downstairs. It was much lighter in the room. A well-to-do neighbor had become

GRACE'S AND THOMAS'S GRAVESTONES

Since the number of seventeenth-century gravestones in the Ipswich cemetery is but a fraction of those who lived in the period, it is fortuitous that those of both Grace and Thomas exist. On Grace's stone the hair around the face is composed of two birds conjoined at the beaks. Several other contemporary stones in the Ipswich cemetery have the same motif. The name Dennis is spelled two different ways. Thomas's stone bears a stylized death's head. The use of design elements—a unique image at the top, similar borders on the edges, and a center panel different from either—is similar to that on Dennis's chests.

interested in old furniture and had come to see the old chest. They admired the old piece. Money changed hands. The chest had been collected. It left the house where it had been since its first owner took it from Thomas Dennis's shop, and it went to another part of town, to the shop of someone who worked on old furniture. There the chest was repaired and cleaned. The flaking paint that had once accented its carving was gone. The top was replaced with a marble slab. The new owner, not wanting to completely do away with the old oak top, had it made into two footstools and a jewelry box. Perhaps this had been the repairman's idea. The chest looked nothing like its former self. At the bottom of the carved center panel, someone had crudely cut the date 1600, right over Thomas Dennis's stamped design.

The chest had a new owner, a local fellow who had become interested in a new pastime, collecting antiques. He and friends around town, many of them men of some means, found virtue in these robust examples of Ipswich's prosperous first century, and a number of pieces of furniture were coaxed from disinterested families. In its new residence, the chest was once again downstairs, this time in the parlor of its new owner. There were several other pieces of joined furniture in the room. They were all bright and shiny; they, too, had been cleaned and polished.

The new owner might go over to the chest and bend down. He put a small key in a new hole in the middle carved panel; it swung open on small hinges, a little door. Thomas Dennis had made those panels to fit tightly into the frame. In fact, all the front panels were now doors, and inside the repairman had put shelves. The collector reached in the middle door, took out a decanter and two glasses, and poured a glass of port for himself and his friend. The chest was now a sideboard, made to fit usefully into the new owner's painfully bright Victorian room. Another life. Many came to see the new owner and to admire his recent acquisition. Other collectors around town and in New England were also pulling furniture from the far corners of dark, old houses, having them cleaned and mended, and displaying them. Some of the old, joined furniture began to turn up in museums.

Then came the chest's last trip—it was bequeathed to the Ipswich Historical Society by the great-granddaughter of the collector and can be seen in the society's seventeenth-century Whipple House. There many visitors saw it, but few asked questions. About twenty-five years ago visitors began to look at it much more. Then ten years ago someone really went at it. He measured it everywhere, drew it, photographed it. Intending to make one just like it, he looked the chest all over, front and back, inside and out, upside down. He shined bright lights on the chest at slight angles. He slowly came to see what the chest could say, he came to read all the marks, the secrets left by Thomas Dennis's shop, the signs of the trees. He made the chest. And then he wrote this book.

Notes

Chapter 1. Ipswich

1. George Francis Dow, ed., *Two Centuries of Travel in Essex County, Massachusetts: A Collection of Narratives and Observations by Travellers, 1605–1799* (Topsfield, Mass.: Topsfield Historical Society, 1921), 6.

2. David Allen Grayson, "*'Vacuum Domicilium'*: The Social and Cultural Landscape of Seventeenth Century New England," in *New England Begins: The Seventeenth Century*, 3 vols., ed. Jonathan Fairbanks and Robert F. Trent (Boston: Museum of Fine Arts, 1982), 1:7.

Chapter 2. Oak

1. James Rosier, "A True Relation of the most Prosperous Voyage made this present year, 1605, by Captain George Weymouth in the Discovery of the Land of Virginia" (London, 1605), in *Chronicles of the Pilgrim Fathers*, ed. Alexander Young (1841; reprint, Boston: Genealogical Publishing Co., 1974), 137.

2. Ipswich Town Records, 1634–1720, 3 vols. (Ipswich, Mass.), 1:10 (hereafter cited as ITR).

3. ITR, 1:157.

4. ITR, 1:154.

5. ITR, 1:306.

6. ITR, 1:338.

7. ITR, 1:169.

8. ITR, 1:201.

9. ITR, 1:269.

10. ITR, 1:229.

Chapter 3. Thomas Dennis in the Woods

1. ITR, 1:300.
2. ITR, 1:10–11.
3. ITR, 1:19.
4. ITR, 1:183–84.
5. Archie N. Frost, ed., *Verbatim transcript of the Records of the Quarterly Courts of Essex County, Massachusetts*, 54 vols. (Salem, Mass.: WPA, 1939), 17:24.1.
6. ITR, 1:300.

Chapter 4. The Town at Work

1. ITR, 1:76.
2. ITR, 1:209.
3. George Francis Dow, ed., *Records and Files of the Quarterly Courts of Essex County, Massachusetts, 1636–1692*, 9 vols. (Salem, Mass.: Essex Institute, 1911–21), 5:37 (hereafter cited as *QCEC*).
4. George Francis Dow, ed., *Probate Records of Essex County, Massachusetts, 1636–1681*, 3 vols. (Salem, Mass.: Essex Institute, 1916–20), 2:191.
5. ITR, 1:329.
6. *QCEC*, 5:304.
7. William Whitmore, ed., *Colonial Laws of Massachusetts* (Boston: Rockwell and Churchill, 1890), 17–18 (hereafter cited as *CLM*).
8. *CLM*, 16–17.
9. *CLM*, 122.
10. ITR, 1:158.
11. *QCEC*, 9:22.
12. *QCEC*, 6:418.
13. *QCEC*, 1:248.
14. *QCEC*, 8:124.

Epilogue

1. *CLM*, 270.

Essay on Method and Sources

The Shop

SOCIAL HISTORIANS typically use documents—manuscripts and printed materials—as their primary sources of data. Some social historians also make use of objects—material culture—mainly from the point of view of the user. There are also historians, epitomized by curators and advanced collectors, who are specialists in classes of objects—furniture, silver, and glass, among many others. These historians also use documents extensively as a way to understand their material, again focused mainly on the user. The look at Thomas Dennis's life has, of course, relied heavily on such sources and could not have been done without them. However, the look here at Thomas Dennis's work relies on quite different sources: the furniture itself, material culture, as informed by the actual making of joined furniture in the shop, hands-on work.

Documents are well understood. The shop, and what can be learned in it, are not so well understood. The shop can be a research tool and even a laboratory. It is possible to do history in the shop. In the case of Thomas Dennis, my work in the shop, and the questions it raised, helped form the questions I asked of the written documents. Others who are doing similar investigations into furniture and other classes of objects will recognize parallels to their own experience. There is, however, no clear methodology of how to proceed. Shop-based research is not taught in universities like the more academic forms of history. It lacks the common language of a discipline. But from others I know who do this sort of shop-based history, there are, in fact, standards of proof that are quite constant across the different crafts. It is perhaps that the three-dimensional, physical reality of the materials and tools, which often will let you do things only one way, teaches one to know when one is right.

Two Tables

One late December day Ted Curtin, my furniture-making partner, brought me the white oak for our next job: two almost identical joined tables for Plimoth Plantation. Since the tables we were reproducing had to look as though they had come from England with the Pilgrims, we used sawn oak. Ted was coming from the mill, where he had a log sawed for this job: 4- by 4-inch legs, 2-inch-thick stuff for the stretchers and aprons. Each of us was to do a table start to finish, so we divided the stock, and I put mine in my mostly unheated shop—a small stove kept the temperature at a comfortable 50 degrees while I worked. By the middle of February the tables were done. They spent the following summer and fall in damp, dirt-floored houses in Plimoth Plantation's Pilgrim Village, where the oak began slowly to dry. After the museum closed, they were moved to a dry, hot storeroom and soon were bone dry. Toward the end of the winter, Ted reported that one of the tables was so loose that a slight push made it sway; the other was as tight as the day it was pinned together. We scratched our heads over that one: we had used oak sawn the same day from the same tree and used the same joinery details. Finally it hit us: one of us had cut the tenons first, been interrupted by a vacation, and at the end chopped the mortises. The other had done just the opposite and sawed the tenons just before assembling the table. The bulb went off: the tenons made early had time to dry and therefore toughen; those made just before assembly were still green and soft: they were too weak to resist the dry draw bore pin, which cut through them like a nail and eliminated the draw bore. This, we realized, was the missing link, the once common bit of knowledge that separated those who worked routinely with green oak from those after: let the tenons dry. We had inadvertently run an experiment. The science of wood technology could have come to the same conclusion, but it had never been asked. For us, the experience of having it happen made it real, and we learned something we never could have by physical examination alone. The loose table, by the way, was no loss. The table was disassembled, the loose pin holes in the tenons plugged, the holes rebored, and the table put back together. A small price for such a lesson.

The Pre-industrial Shop

The pre-industrial shop is different from a modern shop. Hand tools developed slowly over millennia and became supremely adapted to the human body. Most were used by one person and developed to work within the strength of one person. How heavy a head? How long a handle? One-handed? Two-handed? Tool traditions around the world are identical at the biomechanical level. In a traditional woodworking shop there are no sounds but those one makes. Saw, plane, chisel, and mallet each make a different noise, of course, and they all come in different sizes and shapes. There are finer distinctions. The same tool might sound different in various species of wood or in green wood and dry wood. One's hearing is always on, and the sense gathers information. And because one holds the tools in one's hands and is using one's body, touch, like hearing, is also gathering information. One hears the different sound the saw makes as it nears a hard knot. One also feels it: the saw starts to slow down, and the arm responds automatically by pushing harder. Sight, of course, tells much and organizes the information from the other senses, but the other senses do jobs that sight alone can not do. The shop is a physical and sensual place, more mind than body.

I knew an elderly carpenter who had trained just before World War II with his carpenter father. Every tool he learned on was a hand tool. When he returned from the Pacific in 1945 and went back to carpentry, the main difference, he said, was that within a few years many hand tools were powered by electricity. The circular saw, fast and very noisy, quickly replaced the handsaw. Now it is routine to wear hearing protection much of the day. But before the war, he told me, experienced carpenters could tell if a new man's saw was dull by the number of strokes he took to saw by hand through a 2 by 4. Those men did not even have to count the strokes— they could hear and recognize the unusual, stop and attend, and then yell to the youngster that his saw wanted sharpening. That is the way it is in a traditional woodworking shop. I hear what my tools are doing and, if someone else is at work, what they are doing, too. The sounds are mainly routine, unremarkable. But hear a sharp sound or the crack of wood, and you are at attention. Almost always one hears the unfortunate noise, like hammer on thumb, before one hears the curse.

Get It Right the Second Time

Ted and I have found (as have others I've talked to who have done similar things) that the quickest way to knowledge of past techniques is to copy an existing piece. First one observes the original, measures, sketches, takes notes and maybe some photographs. This can take several hours to a day, which is what Ted and I need to do a large, complex piece. Then one makes the piece and compares the replication with the original. One sees things in the original one had not seen before. One makes another piece, sees a little more at the outset, and goes a little further. Gradually the unseen becomes clear: the selection of stock, the engineering of the joinery, the layout, the work sequence, the tools and their marks. When one finally clicks on a shop's particular way of doing things, the whole process becomes transparent: the habitual actions, the solutions to a problem. A cluster of similar working methods is a shop tradition, handed from master to apprentice throughout the generations. Like Thomas Dennis, I have learned the different sounds made in green or dry oak by planing, chopping, and sawing; I know which tools to use when, I can rummage with him through a pile of bolts, and I can split, rive, and shape to his specifications.

One learns another skill: how to see what one is not looking for. One tends to see what one is looking for, which is generally what one knows. But guaranteed there is evidence on a piece that one does not see because one does not yet know that it is evidence. Beginners do not yet know what they do not know, and they miss much evidence. After a while, one understands that there are things yet to be understood and proceeds with more care, speed, and efficiency. A good visual memory helps here, and often one remembers months later something seen on another piece. Also useful are complete field photographs: all sides, many details. This allowed me to figure out, when making a southeastern Massachusetts press cupboard, that the characteristic triangular dentil work on the molding below the top of the bottom section was not carefully laid out but rather was quickly done by stepping a chisel across the molding by eye. Photographs of each end showed that one end had more triangles than the other. This quick application of decoration is typical of the speed with which the joiner worked. Again, the shop drove the observation. If I had not been making the piece, I would not have asked the question. This sequence of gradual insight has led to an aphorism for advancing in the recovery of lost techniques: Get it right the second time.

Field Work

For a few years I lived in an eastern Massachusetts town with an active program of municipal forestry. I arranged to purchase a standing oak of my choice for my furniture. I looked for a large, straight-grained tree with no knots. The tree I chose was in a lot I knew well. In the 20 or so acres of woodlot were a few dead oak snags: the main trunk and the stubs of a few bottom branches were all that was left, and the bark had peeled off. Under the bark, the grain spiraled like a barber's pole. The oak I chose grew from an old fence line on a slight hill. Hence, the bottom few feet of the tree had a slight, gentle curve. The first branch was 25 feet off the ground. I expected some difficult wood at the bottom, but at more than 20 inches in diameter a few feet off the ground it was a large tree. I judged the grain by the bark: by sighting up the fissures one can guess the probable twist in the wood, as the fissures in the bark generally follow the grain. The bark was straight. The tree fell right where it should have, and I began to split the bottom 8-foot log. I could barely get a sharp wedge in the end grain. Finally, I got two started and began to put wedges in the emerging split along the side of the log. This all took the better part of an hour: I had never worked on a log so difficult to split. I went home to get some more wedges. Finally, all my wedges in this one short log, it yielded and I saw what was going on. The tree was as twisted as the old hulks I had seen. And, every twenty to thirty years, the twist reversed direction, and the grain at these spots had to be torn apart. The wood was all but unusable, expensive firewood. I stripped the bark off a section of the log and looked at the rays, those planes of natural cleavage that show up on the outside of the tree's wood. There, under the bark, grain spiraled, yet the bark indicated the grain would be straight. Experience had taught me that the bark was a good clue, but I was wrong. Three hundred years ago, artisans in those woods would not have made the mistake I made: they would have known the trees intimately and probably shared information. A wheelwright would have gladly used my split-resisting tree and by sawing it into thick planks would have avoided my difficulties. But I did not know what I did not know.

The Characteristics of the Dennis Shop

I have learned that making an "exact" replica of a piece proceeds in stages. No matter how thorough the original examination—the measurements, the field notes, and the photographs—there is always something one is not quite sure about. And with a more complex piece, it is likely that many details have to be rechecked. When I made the Dennis chest, I could not have it in the shop with me (the ideal situation), but it was not far away, and I made several trips to see it. It was the first of the Dennis pieces I examined in close detail, and I used it to hone my eye for Dennis work. Then I looked at all the other known Dennis pieces. After I had seen everything, I went back to the first one and saw even more. But the making drove the questions even further.

I took measurements of the length, width, and thickness of all framing pieces at both ends, something I routinely do with joined furniture. Many pieces are not the same dimensions at each end. This indicates the degree of tolerance the joiner, and presumably the client, accepted. Some furniture is extremely precise in the sizing of its boards, and some is less so. The Dennis furniture is in the middle. The lengths of the pieces are precise; the width varies by no more than ¹⁄₁₆ inch. Many of the muntins, however, taper in thickness, and one barely contains the panel groove. This shows Dennis getting as much as he could out of his stock. Many of the pieces had worm holes that were in the tree before Dennis made the chest. Five of the seven pieces that make up the rear of the chest have worm holes, but only one piece on the front. Dennis, it seems, intentionally placed the wormy pieces in the rear.

When I made the replica, I did not copy each piece exactly but worked to Dennis's tolerances. In many places, Dennis used marginal stock, but not where one would notice. I also had the opportunity to use an Ipswich white oak tree. Like the oak in Dennis's furniture, my tree had the occasional worm hole, and some of the insects were in the tree when I split it. It was a bit small, so I had to get the panels from another white oak. So I rived the stock to his tolerances and dressed the stock to his tolerances.

Making the replica of the Dennis chest was research itself: it led me to ask questions other historians do not ask, and hence there is little in print on these minute technical matters. I had to look at all the Dennis pieces to see the cluster of key traits that distinguished the Dennis shop. I had to compare this with what I know of other New England joinery traditions. As a whole, all the New England traditions are extraordinarily similar (much more so than would be the cabinetwork traditions of the eighteenth century). The realities of working in green, riven oak made their own demands. The English tradition from which New England joinery derived was also quite uniform. Differences between regions were mainly in decoration and to a lesser degree in form; these differences are the usual territory of furniture historians. The English tradition itself is similar at the level of the joinery to the joined oak furniture of the rest of northwestern Europe—Dutch, Flemish, and North German.

Thomas Dennis's son and grandson would have to figure out for themselves how to make the transition to cabinetwork: there was no ancient, inherited body of tradition. They probably did much of their figuring out by looking at the work of English-trained immigrant cabinetmakers in Boston and seeing imported furniture, especially when they were in danger of losing their clientele to cabinetwork. The joiners in Ipswich could have seen the same pieces of furniture in town and no doubt other work in Boston, whose wealthier population bought the latest fashions from England. The joiners in any village looked at one another's solutions and learned, and a townwide set of techniques developed. The same thing was going on independently in many regions of New England. It is curious that there are few structural failures in joined furniture but a number of characteristic ones in cabinetwork in the eighteenth century, as American woodworkers tried to solve new technical problems instantly, without the benefit of several centuries of experience.

Dennis's Shop Conventions

The characteristics of the Dennis shop are things I needed to know to make the piece. They are not, by and large, things the client would have stipulated or even noticed. Their consistency indicates a shop tradition, and the exceptions show how complex a small, rural shop could be. First I needed to know the size of the mortise, since I would need a chisel of that width. I had come to view the 5⁄16-inch-wide mortise as the norm, with ¼ inch and ⅜ inch also common. The limiting factor was the strength of the tenon behind the draw bore hole: if the tenon was too short or too thin, the wood could fail behind the pin, neutralizing the draw bore (this is basically what happened to the loose table). Tenons seem everywhere to be an invariable 1¼–1½ inches long, a dimension so widely diffused that it may have been determined as adequate early in the development of joined furniture. So, I argued, any thickness between ¼ and ⅜ inch was adequate. The Ipswich Historical Society's chest, however, used ½-inch mortises to join the horizontals to the stiles. The front edge of the mortises was set back ½ inch from the front face of the stiles, rails, and muntins. I had not seen this large a mortise and tenon joint on any joined oak case furniture. In two-thirds (twelve of seventeen) of the extant Dennis chests I examined that used this large mortise and tenon for the rails, the muntins used a smaller 5⁄16-inch mortise and tenon, set back 5⁄16–⅜ inch from the front faces. This trick let Dennis use thinner stock for the muntins. For these pieces the joiner used two different mortise chisels and marking gauges. Since a 5⁄16- or ⅜-inch mortise and tenon would have been adequate, Dennis's use of the 7⁄16- to ½-inch mortise and tenon, combined with the smaller mortise and tenon, is a distinct shop characteristic: the Dennis shop measurements were internally consistent and distinct from those of other shops.

The other typical characteristics are not quite so unique—they are found in other work—but taken together are highly significant because of their consistency:

Stiles: The stiles (legs) of most Dennis chests are rectangular, 1¾–2 inches thick and 3¼–3⅞ inches wide. Although this rectangular shape is by far the commonest and includes the entire main group, Dennis sometimes used a five-sided stile, the fifth plane being a wide bevel on the inside. This stile shape allowed the joiner to use a much smaller piece of riven oak than he would have needed for a rectangular stile. This five-sided shape is common on southeastern Massachusetts joined oak furniture and almost universal on the Connecticut River Valley furniture.

Till: The top of the typical Dennis till (the small wooden box built into the inside of a chest or box) is slanted. Many boxes also attributable to Dennis have slanted till tops. There are, however, some Dennis pieces with flat-topped tills, the most common sort in general.

Chest bottoms: A core group of six chests uses the same technique: the bottom boards are thin, riven oak boards running front to back, connected along their edges by a tongue and groove. They fit into a groove in the front rail, a rabbet in the end rails, and are nailed into the bottom of the rear rail. They are also fitted neatly into rectangular notches in the rear stiles. To make installation and repair simpler, the bottoms of all chests are typically nailed into the bottom of the rear rail. However, the front and side rails use several methods. Most commonly the side rails have just a rabbet at the bottom edge into which the bottom boards were nailed. Often the fronts of the boards fit into a groove in the front rails (as with the Dennis chests), but sometimes there is just a rabbet in the front rail. The consistency of the Dennis chest bottoms is highly characteristic.

Chest backs: The backs of Dennis's chests are also similar and, as with the bottoms, are made of a consistent set of possible choices. First, the fair, or layout, face of the back of the chest is on the outside, like the other three faces. This seems to be the norm in the New World, although another less common method lays out the fair face of the back of the chest from the inside. All panels made from riven stock have one flat face and one face with a rounded bulge, an artifact of processing the split stock. Universally, the fronts and ends of New England joined chests place the flat face out and the rounded face in, consistent with the general layout technique of letting any irregularities occur on the inside. In most chests the fair face of the rear panels looks out, as on the fronts and ends, but in the Dennis chests the flat face of the rear panels faces in. The effect is that when one opens the chest and looks in, the best face of the rear panels faces the viewer.

Chest tops: The core group uses mainly oak, but pine also occurs. Oak tops are made of three long boards the full length of the chest, about 4½ feet. The tops of some chests are replacements, but originals in both oak and pine exist. The Dennis oak top—three long, riven boards—represents, by my estimate, about six hours of labor more than a single, wide pine board top. The decision to use the oak boards was probably cost-related and the choice of the client. Most extant New England chests use pine tops. Only a few, like Dennis's, use oak board tops.

This complex of details—the mortise and tenon size, the stile section, the till, back, and bottoms—is the core of Dennis's shop tradition. Chests in this group (and the two great chairs) appear to have been carved by the same hand, assumed to be Dennis's; the carving is well executed; and the designs are complex. Another group of chests is equally completely carved, but the panels are carved in rote geometric forms that preclude the necessity of designing to fill the spaces. This group could have been carved by Dennis, or by a son, manually competent but unfamiliar with the finer details of design.

Six chests use a different size mortise and tenon. Two chests have a $\frac{5}{16}$-inch mortise and tenon, and two, a $\frac{3}{8}$-inch one. The two chests with the $\frac{5}{16}$-inch mortise have complex and well-executed carving that was probably done by Dennis. The chests themselves could be the work of a journeyman who brought his habitual ways of working to Dennis's shop. Dennis may have had his journeyman make the chest but carved it himself. To denote a maker of any given piece of furniture, even in a small shop such as Dennis's, is difficult. Three individuals could have worked on a single piece: an apprentice rived and dressed the stock, a journeyman joined the piece, and the master carved it.

If the ½-inch mortise is indeed a sign of Dennis's shop tradition, then it should be found both before and after Dennis. Prior examples could be found among Ottery St. Mary pieces in England, but no search has been undertaken. The Wadsworth Athenaeum has an Ottery St. Mary chest, purchased because the carving is quite similar to that of the museum's Dennis chest, one of the two with the $\frac{5}{16}$-inch mortise and tenon but probably carved by Dennis. However, the Athenaeum's Ottery St. Mary chest uses the $\frac{5}{16}$-inch mortise and tenon and is therefore likely not a product of the shop in which Dennis trained.

There are several other chests in the Dennis group that use some mannerist moldings and applied turnings. These are either later work of Dennis's or the work of one of his sons. This entire group uses the ½-inch mortise. In addition, an Ipswich joined chest of drawers at Winterthur Museum, known as the "Vocabulary" chest, uses both the large and the small mortise and tenon. Without any carving, these chests are more difficult to assign to a given maker. But indications are that the large ½-inch mortise did carry through the generations in Ipswich, and it is quite possible that there are yet to be identified many uncarved, post–Thomas Dennis shop pieces of furniture made by Dennis's sons and even grandson that use this characteristic.

Shop-Related Books

When hands-on work in the shop is the goal, books (and some magazines) are often quite useful. Early in one's hands-on experience playing with wood, one realizes that there are things one does not know. A bit further on, tired of learning by trial and error, one also tires of reinventing the wheel. Suddenly one realizes that someone knows the answer to the problem. If there is no one to talk to (the traditional way to pass such knowledge), one can often find help in printed material, as well as on video, television, and the Internet. The books I mention here are standard ones and widely available.

The first category is books about tools, useful at first for identification and later as reference. The books mentioned here are among the most useful and available of a large number. The American Henry Mercer's *American Carpenters' Tools* (1929; reprint, Doylestown, Pa.: Bucks County Historical Society, 1960) and the British William Goodman's *The History of Woodworking Tools* (London: G. Bell, 1964) are early but easily available standard treatments. R. A. Salamon's *Dictionary of Tools Used in the Woodworking and Allied Trades, c. 1700–1970* (London: Allen and Unwin, 1975) is recent and compendious. A recent, specialized study is Jay Gaynor and Nancy Hagedorn's *Tools: Working Wood in Eighteenth Century America* (Williamsburg, Va.: Colonial Williamsburg Foundation, 1993). Besides these books, the Early American Industries Association, an organization of tool collectors and tool historians, has a lengthy history of publication.

A second category is books on objects, the things made by the tools. Wallace Nutting's *Furniture of the Pilgrim Century,* 2 vols. (1924; reprint, New York: Dover Press, 1965) contains more than fifteen hundred illustrations and is a standard visual reference for American joined furniture. The standard English work, also highly illustrated, is Victor Chinnery's *Oak Furniture: The British Tradition* (Woodbridge, Suffolk: Antique Collectors' Club, 1986). For seventeenth-century material culture, Jonathan Fairbanks and Robert F. Trent's *New England Begins* (Boston: Museum of Fine Arts, 1982) is hard to find but unmatched. Well-illustrated specialized views of other furniture traditions, notable for the way they combine the furniture with the larger cultural context, are Lon Taylor and Dessa Bokides's *New Mexican Furniture, 1600–1940* (Santa Fe: Museum of New Mexico Press, 1987) and Jean Burks and Timothy Rieman's *The Complete Book of Shaker Furniture* (New York: Harry Abrams, 1993). For those interested in digging deeper into seventeenth-century furniture, the many articles of Robert F. Trent are worth finding. For carpentry and early New England timber framing, the best book by far (and a classic of American vernacular architecture) is Abbott Lowell Cummings's *The Framed Houses of Massachusetts Bay* (Cambridge: Harvard University Press, 1979).

A third category is how-to books. The earliest book in English is also one of the best: Joseph Moxon's *Mechanick Exercises* (1703; reprint, Scarsdale, N.Y.: Early American Industries Association, 1979). The text describes the use of joiners' and carpenters' tools in detail. There are many recent how-to books about traditional shop woodworking, many of which are excellent, but a classic is Charles Hayward's *Woodwork Joints* (New York: Drake, 1970). This mid-twentieth-century text of standard and classic English traditions derives directly from Moxon. For traditional rural woodworking, see any of the books by Roy Underhill or Drew Langsner.

The final category is books about other woodworking shops. These are useful not so much for the technical information that they contain as for the social history; they help put the techniques into the larger context of the artisan and his community. Two first-person works by English authors stand out: George Sturt's *The Wheelwrights's Shop* (Cambridge: Cambridge University Press, 1923) and Walter Rose's *The Village Carpenter* (Cambridge: Cambridge University Press, 1937). These authors are, respectively, the owner of a family wheelwright shop and the owner of a rural woodshop, both men largely untouched by the industrial world around them. Their intimate relationship with their local customers and with the local landscape is obvious. A third book, the work of a contemporary scholar, could equally belong with the tool books: Charles Hummel's *With Hammer in Hand* (Charlottesville: University Press of Virginia for the Henry Francis du Pont Winterthur Museum, 1968), about a three-generation pre-industrial shop on Long Island.

Manuscript Sources

A remarkable assortment of written documents pertain to Thomas Dennis, from colonywide laws to pieces of paper he carried in his own pocket. The English who settled in the Massachusetts Bay Colony came from a tradition of record keeping and merely continued in the New World. And the records, housed at the colony/state, county, town, and personal levels—there is a certain amount of luck here—have survived the occasional fire, the cause of most document loss.

At the colony level—a macro view—the complete records of the General Court provide the context for Ipswich and for Dennis, inherent in the laws under which all lived. In 1854 Nathaniel Shurtleff edited *The Records of the Governor and Company of the Massachusetts Bay in New England, 1628–86*, 5 vols. (Boston: W. White, printer to the Commonwealth). Shurtleff's edition contains all the business of the General Court, which includes grants of land and legal proceedings, as well as the laws enacted by the court. The laws alone were edited by William Whitmore as *The Colonial Laws of Massachusetts* (Boston: Rockwell and Churchill, 1890).

Many different records exist at the county level. The court records are complete and contain a tremendous amount of data. A complex case could take many pages of charges and countercharges, and often lengthy and complex depositions, in which one can sometimes hear in a scribe's spelling the dialect of the speaker. The Essex County probate records—wills and inventories—are a second group of useful public records. Social historians in particular have long known of the valuable information contained in the seemingly mundane recording of an individual's possessions. One can often follow those taking the inventory through the house, pausing in each room to list, and value, the items.

Essex County was fortunate to have competent local historians beginning in the nineteenth century. Most prominent is George Francis Dow, who between 1911 and 1921 edited nine volumes, each about five hundred pages, as *The Records and Files of the Quarterly Courts of Essex County, Massachusetts, 1636–1692* (Salem, Mass.: Essex Institute). Dow also edited, between 1916 and 1920, the three-volume set *Probate Record of Essex County, Massachusetts, 1635–1681* (Salem, Mass.: Essex Institute). Dow's editions of the court and probate records are carefully and completely indexed: all references to every name and object can be found, a boon for later historians. Like all who struggle with seventeenth-century handwriting, Dow did make the occasional error, like misreading "Thomas Davis" as "Thomas Dennis." Davis was in court because he had stolen many pounds of nails from a ship in the harbor, but modern historians have blamed Dennis for the act. But Dow can generally be trusted.

Dow worked from the original manuscripts, some of them detailed and lengthy, some of them just scraps of paper with a few words stuffed into the case folder. Under the auspices of the Works Progress Administration a typescript of the complete records was produced, known as the *Verbatim Transcript of the Records of the Quarterly Courts of Essex County, Massachusetts* (Salem, Mass.: 1939), compiled under the supervision of Archie N. Frost, clerk of the courts in Salem, Massachusetts. The fifty-four volumes of the original typescript are in the collections of the Essex Institute in Salem. The typescript is complete and is indexed for names; occasionally it can add small bits to the Dennis story.

At the local level, the Ipswich Town Records are complete and can be conveniently used in a wonderfully clear, well-indexed, handwritten copy made in 1890 by Nathaniel R. Farley. The three volumes, more than one thousand pages, cover the period 1634–1720 and are housed in the Ipswich town clerk's office. All regulations passed by the town are in the records, as are many small matters. Dennis is at times a frequent figure. Ipswich was also fortunate to have had the Reverend Thomas Franklin Waters, arguably the best of his generation of local historians. Waters wrote a massive and accurate two-part history of the town, *Ipswich in the Massachusetts Bay Colony* (Ipswich, Mass.: Ipswich Historical Society, 1905). The first part of the first volume is a general history of seventeenth-century Ipswich; the second part is the history of each of the original Ipswich house lots. Waters used the Ipswich deeds kept then in the Essex County courthouse in Salem. It was a massive job and involved thousands of deeds. Without Waters's work I could not have reconstructed Dennis's Ipswich.

Finally, at the micro level, are the Dennis family papers, with detailed information pertaining to Thomas Dennis, such as the relative net worth of a typical quarter of the Ipswich population in 1690 and the sorts of things a widow might charge with the merchant. Many generations of Dennis males kept the assortment of papers in a carved oak box, made by Thomas. The box is now in the Bowdoin College Museum, and the papers are at the Massachusetts Historical Society.

Index

Clarke, Thomas (carpenter), 76
cleave, 26
Cobbitt, Mrs. (minister's wife), 82
Cobbitt, Thomas (minister), 56
cod fishery, 7, 8
Cogswell, William (husbandman), 58
common field, 9
coopers, 16, 42, 61, 71–72, **73**, 74–76;
     types of oak used by, 51, 72
coppice, 20–22, 26; smallwood in,
     22; standard trees in, **21**, 21–22

Dane, Philemon (physician), 71
Davis, John (joiner), 84, 86
Deare, Edward (turner), 81–82
Denison, Daniel, 46
Dennis, Grace, 59, 88–89, 97, 100;
     gravestone of, **129**
Dennis, John (joiner), 84, 94–95
Dennis, Thomas (joiner), 82, 84,
     86–87, 88; accused by Josias Lyn-
     don, 55; as artisan, 63; carving
     inspiration of, 114–15, **115**, 117;
     carving style of, 15; characteristics
     of furniture produced by, 140–45;
     charged with illegal felling, 55–56,
     58–59; community expectations
     of, 43; gravestone of, **129**; and
     immigration to Ipswich, 14; and
     prosecution by selectmen, 55–56,
     58–59; public service of, 126;
     and visualization of wood in tree,
     42, **101**; in woods in England, 48,
     50; in woods in Ipswich, 42,
     48–51
Dennis, Thomas, Jr. (joiner), 84,
     94–95
Douglas, William (cooper), 74–75
draft animals: horses, 78–79;
     oxen, 78–79
Dutch, Robert (ship owner), 61

Emery, John (carpenter), 86–87
Emery, John, Jr. (joiner), 86
Emery, Jonathan (carpenter), 86–87
enclosed field agriculture, 8–9

felloe, 7, 77
Fellows, William (husbandman), 55;
     farm of, 43, 48, 51
fencing: amount of wood needed for,
     46; need for in Ipswich, 44; pale
     fence, 46–47; rail fence, 47; and
     standards of sufficiency, 47, 86
firewood: Ipswich regulation of, 33,
     34–35; Ipswich usage of, 36
forest, as legal entity in England, 24
Foster, Isaac (wheelwright), 39
freeman, 11
Fuller, Joseph (carpenter), 82
fulling mill, 10

Gaines, John (shoemaker), 82
Gaines, John, Jr. (turner), 82
gauger of cask, 72
General Court, 58
Giddings, George (husbandman,
     turner), 82
glue, 5
great migration, 8, 9
green wood, working with, 97, 98,
     106; in chair construction, 80
gristmill, 10
growth rings, 4, 104; for making
     pins, 124

Hart, Thomas (tanner), 55
hedge, 9, 23, **25**, 44
High Street, Ipswich, 39
Hovey, Daniel (husbandman), 76
Hovey, James (cooper), 76
Howlett, Thomas (carpenter), 62, 66
husbandry, 43, **85**, 86–87

Lord, Robert, Jr. (blacksmith), 56
Low, John (cooper, malt kiln owner), 75, 76
Lower Falls, Ipswich, 10
Lyndon, Josias, 51–57

mannerism, **123**
Massachusetts Bay Colony, 9, 11, 56; General Court of, 11
Mayflower, 8
Merchant, William (husbandman), 39, 44
Mile River, Ipswich, 43

Newbury, 60, 86
Newfoundland, 86
Newmarch, John (blacksmith), 75
Norton, Freegrace (carpenter, miller), 69–71, 78, 80

oak (in England): growing conditions for, 20–28; uses of, 18–20, 26
oak, red, 72
oak, white (in New England): for coopers, 99; differences in splitting of between Old England and New England, 50; for felloes, 78; as fencing material, 32; for firewood, 32; grain of sought by Thomas Dennis, 42; and grant for pails and measures, 66; for pipestaves, 33; presence of in New England, 28–29; pressures on supply of, 32; and regulations regarding Ipswich commons, 32–42, 36–37, 38; smell of, 94; and type of tree sought by Thomas Dennis, 50; use of revived by Arts and Crafts movement, 127; uses of in New England, 28; waste of by Ipswich commoners, 33; for watertight casks, 72

ogee, 113
open field agriculture, 8, 9
orchards, 44
ordinary, 56, 99
Ottery St. Mary, Devonshire, England, 50, 113–14, 122

packer (of casks), 72
Paine, William (attorney), 59
paint, 4; black, 124; vermillion, 124
park land, 23–24, 29
Pengry, Moses (shipyard owner, ordinary keeper), 56, 62, 70–71, 89
penistone, 58
pew end (in Ottery St. Mary), 114, **115**, 116
pipestaves, regulation of, 74
plane shavings, 100
Plymouth, 8
pollard, 26, **27**

rays, **53**, 55
Roper, Nathaniel (carpenter), 66
Roper, Walter (carpenter), 65–66, 67, 68, 71, 74
Rowley, 70

Safford, John (blacksmith), 89
Salem, 9, 84
Saltonstall, Richard (gristmill owner), 70
sawmill: in Chebacco, 65, 67; in Ipswich, 65
Searle, William (joiner), 82, 84, 88–89
small causes, 58
Smith, John (captain), 7, 10, 28, 30
South Commons, Ipswich, 44, 47
Spark, John (ordinary keeper, innkeeper), 65–66, 70
spokes, 77

staves, 51
Story, Seth (carpenter, sawmill owner), 68
Story, William (carpenter), 68–69; as grain and fulling mill owner, 68
Story, William, Jr. (carpenter?), 68

tannery, 89
Tawley, John (merchant), 84, 86
thatch, 69
Tilton, Abraham (carpenter), 71
Tilton, Abraham, Jr. (carpenter), 71, 84
Timber Hill, Ipswich, 38
timber/wood distinction, 22
tools: awl, 102, 103, 117; ax, 42, 44, **64**; beetle (*see also* splitting maul *below*), 52, **64**; bench dog, **83**, 97; bowl lathe, 79; carving gouge, **83**, 118, **119**; dividers, **83**, **90**, 91, 117; fore plane, **83**, **90**, 91, 97, 99; froe, **90**, 91; gimlet, **90**, 91, 111–12; great wheel lathe, 81; hand saw, **83**, 90, 91, 96; hewing hatchet, **83**, **90**, 91, 95, 96, 104; holdfast, **83**, 105, 106, 107; joiner's bench, **83**, 97–98, 105; joiner's shop, **83**, 88; mallet, 107; marking gauge, **90**, 91, 103–5; molding plane, **83**, 113; mortise chisel, **90**, 91, 105, 107–8; paring chisel, **83**, **90**, 91, 106–7; pitsaw, 26, 52, 65; plow plane, 108–9; pole lathe, 80–81, **83**; punch, 121, 123; rabbet plane, **83**, 111; ruler, 97, 98; scratch stock, 113; smooth plane, **90**, 91, 98; spindle lathe, 80; splitting maul, 52, 54; treadle lathe, 81; V tool, 119, 121–23; wedge, 52, 54, 55, **64**; whip saw, 52, **64**

tool marks, **3**, 4, **104**
Treadwell, Nathaniel (blacksmith), 55
tree grants: to artisans, 40; to carpenters, 39–40; for charcoal, 41; to commoners, 38–41; for fencing, 40; for malting, 41
tumbrel, 78
turners, 42, 79–82

Upper Falls, Ipswich, 10, 43, 65

Varnum, George (husbandman), 78
vermillion, 4, 124
viewer of pipestaves, 74

Wade, Jonathan (sawmill owner), 65
wagon, 78
wainscot, 19, 82
Wainwright, Francis (merchant), 58
Waite, Thomas (carpenter, miller), 70, 82
Waite, Thomas, Jr. (carpenter), 82
Wardell, Elihu (carpenter), 67, 71
West End, Ipswich, 60, 79, 81
wheel: construction of, 77–78; dish in, 77; parts of, 77
wheelwrights, 16, 42, 77–79; as makers of farm implements, 79; type of wood sought by, 51
Whipple, Joseph (joiner), 84
Williams, Roger, 30–31
Wilson, Sherburne (cooper), 74–76, 88
Wilson, Theophilus (carpenter), 82
Winthrop, John, 10
Winthrop, John, Jr., 10
Wood, Obadiah (baker), 89
wood pasture, 23–25
Woodward, Ezekiel (carpenter), 67